THE ENCHANTED WORLD OF HONEY MOON™

SHADES AND SHENANIGANS

by
Suzanne Brooks Kuhn

Created by Mark Andrew Poe

Illustrations by Becky Minor
Based on the artwork of Christina Weidman

rabbit publishers

Shades and Shenanigans (The Enchanted World of Honey Moon),
by Suzanne Brooks Kuhn
Created by Mark Andrew Poe

Rabbit Publishers
1624 W. Northwest Highway
Arlington Heights, IL 60004

Illustrations by Becky Minor
  Based on the artwork of Christina Weidman
Cover and Interior Design by Lewis Design & Marketing

ISBN: 978-1-943785-16-2

10 9 8 7 6 5 4 3 2 1

1. Fiction - Action and Adventure 2. Children's Fiction
First Edition
Printed in U.S.A.

Stay the course, Honey Moon.
Stay the course.

TABLE OF CONTENTS

PREFACE

Halloween visited the little town of Sleepy Hollow and never left. Many moons ago, a sly and evil mayor found the powers of darkness helpful in building Sleepy Hollow into "Spooky Town," one of the country's most celebrated attractions. Now, years later, the indomitable Honey Moon understands she must live in the town but she doesn't have to like it and she is doing everything she can to make sure that goodness and light are more important than evil and darkness.

Welcome to *The Enchanted World of Honey Moon*. Halloween may have found a home in Sleepy Hollow, but Honey and her friends are going to make sure it doesn't catch them in its Spooky Town web.

FAMILY

Honey Moon

Honey is ten-years-old. She is in the fifth grade at Sleepy Hollow Elementary School. She loves to read and she loves to spend time with her friends. Honey is sassy and spirited and doesn't have any trouble speaking her mind—even if it gets her grounded once in a while. Honey has a strong sensor when it comes to knowing right from wrong and good from evil and like she says, when it comes to doing the right thing— Honey goes where she is needed.

Harry Moon

Harry is Honey's older brother. He is thirteen years old and in the eighth grade at Sleepy Hollow Middle School. Harry is a magician. And not just a kid magician who does kid tricks, nope, Harry has the true gift of magic.

Harvest Moon

Harvest is the baby of the Moon family. He is two-years-old. Sometimes Honey has to watch him but she mostly doesn't mind.

Mary Moon

Mary Moon is the mom. She is fair and straightforward with her kids. She loves them dearly and they know it. Mary works full-time as a nurse, so she often relies on her family for help around the house.

John Moon

John is the dad. He's a bit of a nerd. He works as an IT professional and sometimes he thinks he would love it if his children followed in his footsteps. But he respects that Harry, Honey and possibly Harvest will need to go their own way. John owns a classic sports car he calls Emma.

Half Moon

Half Moon is the family dog. He is big and clumsy and has floppy ears. Half is pretty much your basic dog.

FRIENDS

Becky Young

Becky is Honey's best friend. They've known each other since pre-school. Becky is quiet and smart. She is an artist. She is loyal to Honey and usually lets Honey take the lead but occasionally Becky makes her thoughts known. And she has really great ideas.

Claire Sinclair

IV

Claire is also Honey's friend. She's a bit bossy, like Honey, so they sometimes clash. Claire is an athlete. She enjoys all sports but especially soccer, softball and basketball. Sometimes kids poke fun at her rhyming name. But she doesn't mind—not one bit.

Brianna Royal

Brianna is also one of Honey's classmates. Brianna is different from all the other kids. She definitely dances to her own music. Brianna is very special. She seems to know things before they happen and always shows up in the nick of time when a friend is in trouble.

FOES

Clarice Maxine Kligore

Clarice is Honey's arch nemesis. For some reason Clarice doesn't like Honey and tries to bully her. But Honey has no trouble standing up to her. The reason Clarice likes to hassle Honey probably has something to do with the fact that Honey knows the truth abut the Kligores. They are evil.

Maximus Kligore

The Honorable (or not-so honorable depending on your viewpoint) Maximus Kligore is the mayor of Sleepy Hollow. He is the one who plunged Sleepy Hollow into a state of eternal Halloween. He said it was just a publicity stunt to raise town revenues and increase jobs. But Honey knows different. She knows there is more to Kligore's plans. Something so much more sinister.

V

ROAD BLOCK

"Honey Moon, you are going to be late for school!"

Her mother's voice snatched her away from the exciting seaside adventure she was reading. How could it be that Honey was lying on her bed in good old, spooky Sleepy Hollow, Massachusetts? In her imagination she'd been on the docks in Bora Bora with Tabby, the dolphin rescuer, as she outwitted the poachers.

"Honey, come downstairs, now!"

Honey glanced at her bedside clock. *Oh no!* She shoved the book into her hideous, turtle-shaped backpack. She'd dressed early so she'd have time to read one more chapter. But one chapter turned to two, to three, and suddenly Mom was calling. She should have already eaten breakfast by now. With the turtle backpack bumping against her shoulders, she dashed downstairs and skidded into the kitchen. She nearly plowed into her big brother, Harry, slurping milk out of his cereal bowl.

"You're late," Mom said. She nodded toward the box of cereal. "I left the Skull Crunchies out for you, but you'll have to hurry." Mom stuffed a sippy cup and a board book into Harvest's diaper bag. Harvest is going to stay with Grandma today while I'm at work and I have to drop him off."

Lucky two-year-old Harvest. Staying with

Grandma was better than going to school.

"Where's Mrs. Wilcox?" Harry asked.

"She called to say she won't be able to take care of Harvest for a while. Her mom is in the hospital. She will be taking a couple of weeks off."

"Oh, okay," Harry said. "I hope she'll be all right."

3

Honey grabbed the cereal box and poured the chocolaty, cereal skulls into her bowl. Not enough time to eat it all, but she hoped she could get enough down to keep her stomach from growling during silent reading time. That only happened one time, but her stomach growled so loud the entire class laughed. And Honey did not want to do a repeat performance.

"Hey, Mom," Harry said. "There wasn't a clean towel in the bathroom this morning when I went to take a shower. I had to use my pajamas to dry off."

Honey shoveled in the Skulls as fast as she could.

"I know," Mom said. "I've been so busy with work, and well, I've been meaning to tell you kids—"

"What?" Honey asked. "You sound serious."
"No, it's a good thing actually. I'm going to need you two to pick up the slack while Mrs. Wilcox is gone."

4

Honey swallowed her chocolaty skulls—hard. "What do you mean?" She did not like the sound of this. Honey lowered her spoon. She looked at Harry and Harry looked at her.

"Like with the laundry. So you don't have to dry off with your PJs," Mom said. "And with vacuuming and dusting. Load the dishwasher."

"I don't know how to start the washer," Harry said. "And I'm kind of booked with magic shows."

Mom sat at the table. "The extra chores will be good for you. It's not negotiable."

"First off," Honey said with a Skull stuck to her chin. "I'm only ten years old. I don't think I'm supposed to operate heavy machinery. And, in case you haven't noticed, I'm not complaining."

Mom zipped up the diaper bag. "We are a family. We take care of each other's problems. There's no reason you can't start doing more chores to help out around the house. And besides, laundry is not a problem—it's life."

"I guess it will be all right," Harry said. "At least on days when I'm not doing my show."

Mom smiled. "You will both survive. I promise. Now get to school."

Half Moon, who was lurking under the table waiting for chocolate skulls to drop let go a soft bark.

"See that," Mom said. "Half agrees."

Harry grabbed his book bag and ran out the door. "See ya."

"But laundry?" Honey said. Why couldn't she do something cool like rescue dolphins from

6

poachers? "Dirty underwear and Harry's smelly tee shirts—ugh."

"We'll figure it out later," Mom said. "Right now you need to get to school and I have to get to Grandma's."

"What's it matter? Why do I need to go to school? I can just stay home and clean the house," Honey said.

Mom took a deep breath and let it out slowly, which usually meant that Honey had pushed too far. "And why shouldn't you clean the house? You live here too. A few extra chores will not kill you—and neither will smelly tee shirts. I'll make a list."

Honey swallowed again. "A list? So now there's a list? Like, how long is this list?"

Mom pulled the diaper bag over her shoulder. "Yes, a list of ways you can be even more helpful around the house." Then she smiled again. "You can be very helpful when you want to be, Honey. And right now the family needs your help."

Harry's DO NO EVIL club was helping others. They did a lot of stuff around town— mowing lawns, carrying groceries, changing light bulbs in high places for some of the older folks. It's what Harry called, "good mischief." Dad was solving problems for people at his IT job, plus he brought home a paycheck to feed them. Ditto Mom. Her job at the hospital was definitely helping others. That left Honey to mess with dirty laundry and vacuum and dust and who knows what else Mom might add to the list.

Sometimes being the middle child was the worst place in the universe.

The only thing worse was if the middle child was tardy to school.

Without another word, Honey grabbed her backpack and stomped to the door.

"Have a nice day, Honey," Mom said. "I'd drive you but Grandma's house is in the other direction and well . . . you made yourself late."

School wasn't far, but Honey always carried too many books so her backpack weighed as much as an anchor, because her greatest fear was to have to wait on someone and not have a book to read. Today, the extra weight slowed her down. "Weight makes late," she said out loud with a chuckle. She picked up the pace as much as she could and by the time Honey reached the school, she was huffing and puffing like Half Moon after a run in the park.

No time to rest. The first bell had rung.

The long hall stretched in front of her. Almost there. She looked to the right, then to the left. No teachers in sight, only a couple of other late kids scurrying into classrooms.

Focusing on the staircase that led to her fifth grade classroom, Honey raced down the corridor. The artwork pinned to the walls fluttered as she sped by. She couldn't believe that Principal Chancellor wasn't in the hall. This was her lucky day. At this speed she'd be in her seat by the second bell. Except for one classroom—the music room. She would need to get past without the teacher seeing her. The music room was not Honey's favorite place. The music teacher, Miss Fortissimo, always seemed to have it out for Honey. She needed to go into ninja mode and sneak past Miss F's room even if it meant making her even tardier.

Honey moved like a cat. She could see the wide stairwell. Just a few more steps then she'd be home free or home-room free. But

9

suddenly four girls wearing black sunglasses poured from Miss Fortissimo's room. Honey barely had time to see the rhinestones that topped the frames of their shades before they turned toward the steps. The steps she needed to go up. Quickly.

Shoulder-to-shoulder they blocked the steps.

"Excuse me," Honey said. "Coming through."

"What was that?" Taylor said. "Did anyone else hear a noise?"

"I didn't hear anything," Clarice Kligore said. She moved closer to Taylor, making the girls' blockade even tighter. "I'm just on a peaceful stroll to get the second graders. Miss Fortissimo arranged for us to do a concert for them."

Clarice was Mayor Kligore's daughter. The mayor and his family pretty much thought they owned Sleepy Hollow.

"It was me, Clarice, and you know it," Honey said. "Let me get through." Honey tried to push her way through but only succeeded in getting her shoulder smashed against the concrete block wall.

"Besides, I don't think queens can even hear when someone who isn't royal is talking to them," Clarice said.

"Come on, Clarice," Honey said. "Get out of the way. I'm going to be late and besides, what did I ever do to you?"

Taylor glared over her shoulder as the girls took another very slow step up the staircase. "You've never done anything for us. That's the problem. We've got our eyes on you."

Ironic since their glasses were so dark they probably couldn't see anything.

BING. BING.

The tardy bell sounded. Honey hadn't reached her classroom yet and already her shirt had come untucked from her skirt and her ponytail had lost some of its sleekness. That's what happened when you got pinned to the concrete wall.

11

The girls weren't satisfied with just making her late. They were trying to win the world record for slowest-moving animal ever.

"I'm flattered that you want to spend more time with me," Honey said. "That must be why you're going so . . . SLOW. Like a bunch of three-toed sloths."

Paige chuckled. Clarice shushed her by putting her blood red fingernail to her blood red lips. Clarice wore makeup already, and it made her look totally fake and even a little scary. No one but a vampire wore those colors...and Betty Tinseltown who did Mom's hair, but she was an old lady.

Honey persisted. "So, if you don't mind me talking to pass the time here, are you some kind of gang?"

"May I answer, Clarice?" Taylor asked.

Honey cringed as Clarice nodded her head and said, "Yes, my minion, you may."

"We're a . . . a club," Taylor said. "We're the

12

Royal Shades. See our sunglasses?" She turned around quickly so Honey could get a better look.

"Yeah," Honey said with a smirk. "Genius. Pure genius wearing them *inside* the building." Even as Honey spoke she was trying to think of some way she could exploit that into a weakness. Dim the lights so they couldn't see at all? Introduce steam into the hallway so the glasses fogged up and she could squeeze past them? Well, that sort of thing only worked for action heroes in the movies. And it wasn't like she could actually do any of that on her way to class. Someday she'd be a hero. Like Harry. But Harry had a friend to help him—a large, Harlequin bunny he called Rabbit. Yeah, it sounded strange even to her but there was no denying that Rabbit was special and that he guided Harry and helped out when need- ed. What Honey needed was a sidekick, or two, or three, if she was ever going to beat Clarice Maxine Kligore at her own game.

They finally reached the first landing and Honey's turtle backpack bounced against her

13

back as a gentle reminder she had better get to class. Honey smiled. Even though he was ugly, Turtle kind of had her back.

"Come on, Clarice, let me go! I'm late!"

But Clarice laughed and snorted air out her nose.

The Royal Shades came to a sudden and complete stop. Honey stopped herself just before she slammed into Clarice. Paige turned around and tapped the frame of her shades. "These glasses are magic. When we wear them we can tell who is . . . danger—"

"Shhh!" Clarice snapped. "You don't know what you're talking about."

Paige's chin dropped. "Sorry," she mumbled.

Honey did not like the sound of it. She knew about magic, the good magic, the real magic that Harry does. And why would they need special sunglasses to show them who is dangerous—at least that was what Honey figured Paige was about to say.

14

Finally, they reached the top of the stairs and two wide doors. Not even the Royal Shades could block Honey here—someone had to open the door. With a smirk, Taylor motioned Honey through their line. "Now that we've escorted you safely to the fifth-grade hallway...."

"Just remember." Clarice grabbed Honey's elbow. "The Royal Shades know who you are. If you help us, we might be able to do something for you too."

15

"I'd rather save a spider from being eaten by a mockingbird." Honey jerked her arm away. "And mockingbirds are my favorite bird."

Clarice lowered her glasses and pinned Honey with cold, blue eyes. "I'll remember that!" Then with a flounce, the four MEAN QUEENS strutted away down the hall.

Royal Shades? More like royal pains in the neck.

Honey dashed down the hallway to her

class. She could hear Mrs. Tenure taking roll through the opened doorway.

Honey slid her backpack off her shoulder. She caught the strap before it hit the floor. She'd have to slink in without Mrs. Tenure noticing.

16

She edged against the doorframe and leaned forward so she wouldn't bump into the intercom with her head. Honey knew from experience that it was practically impossible to sneak into her classroom without accidentally paging the office. Fortunately, Honey's desk was on this side of the classroom. Honey slinked another two steps when she caught Brianna's eye. Everyone else was looking straight ahead at Mrs. Tenure, who had no patience with homeroom shenanigans. Brianna's chair sat at the back, a little removed from everyone else's. Her pink tutu was squished by her chair. *Another costume?* But that was Brianna. Honey tiptoed toward her seat.

"Madeline? Emily? Aiden?" Mrs. Tenure read. Good, she was still in the H through L section. She hadn't reached the M's yet. Just a few more feet.

"Honey?"

Honey wasn't quite to her seat, but she did her best to throw her voice. "Here."

Mrs. Tenure looked up from her roll book. "But you weren't here at the bell, were you?"

"No, Mrs. Tenure. Sorry . . . but ... but I was reading and got caught up in the stor—"

17

"That'll be 100 sentences for you to turn in tomorrow," Mrs. Tenure said. "I'll think of something nice and long for you, because I know how you like big words."

The class snickered but Mrs. Tenure quickly silenced them with only a look.

Words, Honey thought. Words like injustice?

Honey already knew that one.

ANOTHER ROAD BLOCK

I will make every attempt to reach class punctually . . . unless blocked by freaky girls wearing sunglasses who have no respect for courtesy.

Mrs. Tenure had chosen the sentence, and although Honey wanted to add the second part, why give herself twice the work? She needed to finish it before Mom found out that she'd gotten in trouble and grounded her. Grounding wouldn't be good today because Honey and her best friend Becky Young were going to play on Claire Sinclair's new trampoline. Becky was the nicest person Honey knew, but Claire Sinclair could be bossy. She thought that just because she could beat Walker and Jacob at soccer, that she was someone special. Well, if Claire got too bossy, Honey would come home and finish reading *Tabby's Dolphin Rescue*. Books didn't block you in the hallways or make you so late to class that you had to write sentences. Honey slid her completed work into her folder. To be honest, it was the book that made her late, but how could you hold a grudge against a good book?

Honey heard her mother in the living room talking to Harvest. Time to be quick. Get out of there before mom asked her to let Harvest play too. Nothing like trying to be cool while your two-year-old brother was smelling up his diaper. She'd just get a drink of juice before she left. Honey eased the refrigerator open and reached for the orange juice carton. It wasn't heavy. About half full, so no one would care if she drank it straight, right?

She lifted the carton to her mouth and slowly tilted it. But before she could take a swig, something on the refrigerator caught her eye.

Under the New York magnet was a picture of a girl her age with big brown eyes. Anisha lived in India and sent them letters every few months. Honey's parents sent a little money to an organization that made it possible for kids in far-away countries go to school. Honey read the letter. It started out with the usual stuff Anisha always wrote, like she was studying math and reading, but then the letter changed. Anisha wrote about how she had to miss school for a while because her mom had been sick and Anisha had to work in the fields during harvest. But now she was back at school and catching up. Imagine! Not being able to go to school. That's the worst.

21

Honey tipped the big carton to her lips and took a medium gulp, but before she could swallow, her eyes landed on something new next to Anisha's letter. A chart. And it had her name on it.

HONEY'S CHORES!

Honey was so surprised she spit the orange juice and bobbled the carton. OJ splashed down her neck. She wiped her face with the back of her hand. Yuck! Honey tossed the now empty carton into the recycle bin.

"Mom!" Honey ripped the paper off the refrigerator, sending the magnet skittering across the floor. "Mom, what's this?" Honey turned toward the living room but her Mom was already standing in the kitchen.

She wore a cowboy hat and a plastic sheriff's badge pinned to her blouse. Honey waved the CHORES paper in front of Mom's face. Evidence of a most foul betrayal. Mom's arms folded over her chest and her face settled into stubborn lines. Lines that Honey recognized as sure trouble.

"That's your chore chart. I told you this morning I was writing a list."

"I can't do chores. I'm too busy. I'm supposed to go to Claire's to bounce on her new trampoline."

"Excuse me, young lady? You are never too busy to take care of yourself. I work forty hours a week and when I'm not on shift I want to spend time with you kids. On my days off, Harvest needs to do more than stand around and watch me fold laundry and clean toilets."

23

She had to be kidding. Honey turned the paper over and stared in horror at the list. Sure enough, there was a line that read, "Tidy Up Kids' Bathroom."

Child labor? Wasn't that illegal? Toilets? Really?

"It's not fair," Honey said. "I work hard at school--harder than the teachers. They just make copies, and I have to solve all their problems. And what do I get? Nothing! And they get a paycheck! And now I'm going to have to work at home." Her eyes narrowed. "Wait a sec. Is there an allowance attached to these duties?" At school she got good grades for hard work. So maybe . . . maybe extra chores had their own reward.

"We'll see how you do," Mom said. "For now it should be enough to know that you're contributing to the family. Let that be your reward."

As far as motivational speakers went, her mother was the worst.

"I'd rather my reward be cold, hard cash. I'd rather get to pick the jobs I do. I'd rather not do anything at all. I need to play too."

Harvest chose that moment to come galloping in on his stick horse. "Yee-haw," he called to Mom.

"Yee-haw, little cowboy," she said. "Maybe after Honey finishes her chores she can take you outside to play."

Honey wiped at her sticky neck. This day could not get any worse. First her mother's big announcement, then the Royal Shades, then writing sentences, then chores, and NOW she had to play with Harvest. And speaking of brothers—

"What about Harry?" Honey asked. A drop of juice trembled on her chin and fell on her shirt. "Does Harry have chores today?"

Mom shook her head. "Harry has to clean up after himself, and he has his own regular and extra chores. But he's got other responsibilities after school today. He's only thirteen but he's got a career, a calling."

A calling. Sometimes Honey got sick of hearing about Harry's calling. But she knew deep down that Harry sometimes did amazing things to help stop some of the Halloween nonsense in Sleepy Hollow.

"Harry is important, but I'm not? I might have a calling too." Although Honey wasn't exactly sure what that could be—Harry did tell her once that she had a really strong sensor when it came to know right from wrong, evil from good, which probably explains why the hair on the back of her neck stood up when she first set eyes on the Royal Shades.

"You're important," said Mom. "And someday you'll figure out your calling. But for now you have to complete that small list of chores and take Harvest with you. After you mop up the juice you spilled on the floor and pre-treat that shirt so it doesn't stain."

"Mom..." Honey wasn't a whiner. Really. She was much more likely to get into trouble for arguing than whining, but there were times when you knew your parents were completely unreasonable and only whining could adequately reach them.

Mom opened the door that went to the garage. She stepped inside and returned with a mop. In her cowboy hat, she looked tougher than the cafeteria's ravioli. The sunlight that burst through the kitchen window caught her sheriff's badge and made it gleam. "Saddle up, pardner," Mom said. "There's work to be done."

Honey took the mop. Harvest clapped his hands causing him to drop his horse. "Mommy's the sheriff. Mommy's the sheriff."

More like an outlaw bandit who stole perfect afternoons from her daughter.

Honey dumped a scoop of Meaty Mummies into Half Moon's empty bowl in the laundry room. "Good old Sleepy Hollow," Honey

said. "Even the dog food is stuck in Halloween."
But just as she turned her back, Half galloped
into the room, tripped over his own four dog
feet and slid, belly first, into the bowl knocking
liver-flavored kibble as far as the eye could see.

"Rats!" Honey shouted. "You clumsy dog."

But Half Moon was used to insults and
proceeded to eat food from the floor—a
floor she would now have to sweep and mop
because it was covered by dog spit.

Honey let go a huge sigh as she grabbed
the mop—again! But all she could do was shake
her head and laugh. Finally, she was finished.

While she'd been sweeping, mopping,
pre-soaking, and filling food bowls, the sun
had moved. Now it was barely over the trees
of her backyard. Soon it'd be time for dinner
and her afternoon of freedom could never be
regained. She squinted into the sun and that
made her think about the Royal Shades. Maybe
she should tell Mom but . . . no, then she'd
have to tell her about being extra late and
writing sentences.

28

"See, that didn't take too long." Mom stirred the peppers in the sizzling skillet. "Go on to Claire's house, but watch the clock. Dinner will be in forty-five minutes."

Forty-five minutes? Honey looked at the peppers already sautéing. Their spicy scent made her stomach growl. "Those are almost ready," she said.

With another scrape of the wooden spoon against the no-stick pan, Mom added, "Take Harvest with you. I can keep supper warm until everyone is home."

"Does he have to wear the cowboy boots?" Honey asked.

Harvest grinned up at her. Well, maybe it was kinda cute.

It only took a minute to walk to the Sinclair's house. But she had to pass the town green where the Headless Horseman statue stood. The statue always gave her the creeps even though it was just bronze and not real. Honey and Harvest had just turned in at Claire's driveway when Honey heard shouts from the backyard. Becky bounced into view over the stockade fence, then disappeared. Claire floated up, then dropped. The trampoline springs squeaked with every bounce.

"We're back -" Becky disappeared again. "- here," she said as she bounced up again.

"The gate is-" Claire dropped out of sight. "- unlocked."

30

Harvest's hand tightened in Honey's. She looked at his face. His eyes grew big. Yeah, he'd love the trampoline. And so would she.

The gate swung open easily, but Honey had to hurry to push Harvest through and close it before Claire's little white dog could scoot out. Harvest laughed delightedly as the pup gave him a good face-washing.

Becky dropped to her bottom and hung her legs over the edge of the trampoline. "What took you so long?"

"Chores," Honey said. "Mom made a new

chore chart. It's ridiculous."

"It must be a lot of chores," Becky said, "Do you have to do them every day?"

"Probably . . . well at least until Mrs. Wilcox comes back," Honey said.

Harvest held his hands up to Honey. "Jump," he said.

"Hold it down, Claire," Honey said. "Let Harvest jump for a minute."

"You aren't my boss." Claire's blond ponytail floated like mermaid hair as she performed another flawless flip.

"Please," Honey said. "We haven't got much time and Harvest really wants to bounce."

Becky hopped off the trampoline. Her dolphin charm bracelet jangled. "It's about time for me to go home anyway. I'm reading book #10 in the dolphin series," she said. "Tabby is rescuing a dolphin that got caught in a fisherman's net. She meets a veterinarian and

I think the veterinarian is going to ask Tabby to help her find the poachers. It's so exciting! You have to read it next."

"I'm still on book #1," Honey said. "Give me some time." Honestly, Honey could probably fly through the books quickly, but she liked to challenge herself by reading several books at a time.

"I want to jump," Harvest said.

"Okay, okay," Honey said.

"Okay, okay," Claire said. "Boy, little brothers can be kind of annoying." But her jumps slowed and soon she was reaching over the edge for Harvest. Honey pulled off his cowboy boots, then picked him up and handed him to Claire. Harvest squealed in delight. He ran around the trampoline, high-stepping and going faster and faster until he fell. But instead of crying, he laughed hysterically.

At least someone was having fun.

32

Placing both hands on the trampoline, Claire bounced Harvest gently. Honey had never seen her act so nice. Maybe someday Claire would be as good of a babysitter as her big sister, Sarah.

"Did you hear about the new club at school?" Claire asked. "Clarice Kligore and Taylor started it."

"Does it have something to do with queens?" Becky asked as she tied her shoes.

33

"They think they're something special," Claire said. "They strut around school like queens. The rules are that they have to wear sunglasses all the time, and they have to do whatever Clarice tells them to.

"I know all about it," Honey said as she climbed onto the trampoline to guard the opposite side. Harvest was getting braver and braver with his jumping. "They blocked my way to class this morning and made me even later for homeroom. I had to write 100 sentences because of them."

"Oh, that explains why you were late." Becky frowned. "We waited for you on the playground before school but we didn't see you.

34

"I was late because I got so interested in the dolphin book. But they didn't let me catch up. I kind of ran into them outside the music room. Clarice told them to link arms and block me. I didn't stand a chance."

"Who'd want to join a club just to get bossed around?" Becky asked. "Don't they get enough of it from their parents? And their teachers?

And their coaches?"

Being a kid meant that everyone got to tell you what to do. It was just another reason Honey couldn't wait to grow up.

Claire bounced high and that made Harvest bounce high. He giggled and landed SPLAT! On his belly.

"I saw Clarice today at lunch," Becky said. "I don't know where you guys were."

"I was at Lunch Bunch in the library," Honey said. "Best part of my day."

"And I was in Coding Club," Claire said.

"Oh yeah," Becky said. "Anyway, Clarice was wearing sunglasses. I thought it was weird and creepy to wear them in the cafeteria."

"That's Sleepy Hollow," Honey said. "Creepy usually rules the day."

"Well, she was sitting with Taylor, D'Shaunte and Paige at a big table, all by themselves."

"But they can't hog tables," Claire said.

"I heard one of the cafeteria monitors say something, but it was really weird, she just backed away from Clarice. Almost like Clarice had some kind of control."

Honey felt the hair on her arms bristle. A sure sign that something was not right.

"But then Brianna sat down at the table. I heard Taylor tell her to leave." Becky had stopped tying her shoes. Her normally happy face creased with worry. "That wasn't nice, was it? Brianna just sat and looked at them. She turned her seat a little to the side, and ate her lunch anyway."

"Good for Brianna," Honey said. You never knew exactly what Brianna would do, but she was glad the girl hadn't given in to the numbskulled bullies.

"I would've flipped their trays over and spilled their nuggets and Jell-O all over the table," said Claire. "And then I'd take their drinks and pour them out in their laps..."

Harvest stopped bouncing. The louder Claire got, the faster his bottom lip quivered.

Honey held out her hands to Harvest. "Don't worry, kid. She's not going to hurt you."

Claire looked only halfway ashamed as he hopped to Honey. "I'm not mad at you, Harvest," Claire said. "But no one tells me where to sit."

Honey felt the same way. She couldn't allow a bully to take over Sleepy Hollow Elementary. She had enough people telling her what to do, she didn't need more.

"Come on, Harvest," she said. "We better get home."

"See you tomorrow," Becky said.

Honey held Harvest's hand as they passed by the Headless Horseman. "Don't let anyone bully you. Tell a teacher or Mom or Dad or me or Harry."

"Rabbit?" Harvest said.

Honey smiled. "Yeah, you can tell Rabbit."

38

RECESS RASCALS

After supper, Honey went to her room. It had been a long day. She had a little math homework but mostly she wanted to read more of her book. Books had a way of taking her far from her troubles and even clearing her mind so she could tackle other things. Maybe even dealing with the Royal Shades.

She reached into her backpack. This time it

was like the turtle was looking straight at her, or maybe even *through* her. "You saw them block me," Honey said. "They were in the wrong. I know they're just a bunch of bullies, but I can't ignore them. I can't."

Honey flopped onto her bed and opened Tabby's Rescue. From somewhere deep inside, a feeling grew and Honey got an idea. Sometimes you had to fight fire with fire. Harry would never agree but Honey had her own way of dealing with evil.

She grabbed Turtle and looked him square in the eyes. "I go where I am needed."

Honey cut her chicken fillet with the black, plastic fork, then smothered it in the lumpy gray stuff they tried to pass off as gravy. "Look at them," she said with a nod toward the Royal Shade's table. "They are taking up the whole table again."

"Brianna isn't sitting with them this time," Becky said. "They are still being mean to her.

40

I saw Clarice talking to her outside the girls' bathroom near the gym. Clarice ran off when she saw me."

"What did Brianna say?" Honey asked.

"Nothing," Becky said. "She smiled at me like she always does and then skipped down the hall."

"I wonder why they want to be mean to Brianna." Claire scooped a spoonful of gravy, then poured it out slowly over the chicken, watching the clumps fall.

Honey shook her head. "I bet you could ask them one hundred times, and they could give you a hundred answers and not one of them would be good," she said.

"I can't believe they are allowed to take a whole table for themselves," Becky said. "The cafeteria monitors just ignore them. It's rude."

"Rude is only the tip of the iceberg lettuce," Honey said.

41

"What if I did ask why a hundred times a day?" Claire said. "Wouldn't that be fun?"

Honey shook her head. "Don't be silly, Claire. Or annoying. Let's change the subject."

Becky swallowed a bite of her PB&J. She always packed a lunch. Sometimes it was weird like hummus and celery or apples and peanut butter or even Sushi. At least Honey thought her lunches were weird.

"I saw you talking to Miss Fortissimo in music," Becky said. "What was that about?"

Honey chewed on another bite of chicken. "I thought she would want to know that they were misbehaving in the hallway."

"Why?" Claire asked with a smile.

"Because she was the one who sent them to get the second graders. If they were causing trouble when they were supposed to be in class, it could come back on Miss Fortissimo."

"Why?" Claire poured another lumpy spoonful of gravy on the chicken.

"Because a teacher is responsible when she sends kids out of the classroom. Next time she might not want to trust them."

Becky pulled a small baggie of carrot sticks from her lunch box. "I'm surprised she chose them anyway. Seems like the sunglasses should be a clue that they were up to no good."

43

"Why?" asked Claire. This time she let go a little chuckle.

Becky shrugged. "Doesn't it seem disrespectful to wear them inside? And all the teachers ignore them. It's weird."

Honey nodded. "Clarice told me they were singing for the second graders, so maybe Miss Fortissimo thought that the sunglasses were part of their costume. But do you know what's even worse?"

"Why?" asked Claire. "I mean what?"

"Miss Fortissimo said I'd better be careful. If I want to keep my straight As, I can't ask too many questions." Honey shivered. "It made me feel a little strange when she said it."

"Why?"

Claire had never seemed so interested in what Honey was saying before. Usually she interrupted to talk about whatever basketball game was being shown on TV that night.

44

"I didn't think about it then but it sounds like she's one of them."

Becky dropped a carrot stick onto the table. "What? But how?"

"And WHY?" Claire said.

Honey's stomach wobbled. "It makes sense, doesn't it? Why else would she protect them?"

Claire nodded and then looked over at the

Royal Shades. "I just got a chill."

"Anyway, I told Miss Fortissimo that they were walking too slow in the hall and I didn't appreciate it. And . . . get this. She just laughed."

"Why?" Of course, it was Claire asking.

But this time Honey glared at her.

"Don't be annoying," Honey said.

45

Becky looked thoughtful and then said, "Well, you're always getting into trouble for running in the halls, she probably didn't see walking slow as an offense."

Honey took a breath and snorted it out her nose. "Nah. There's more to this. I can feel it."

"Let's go outside," Honey said as she took her last bite of dry chicken strips.

"Why?" asked Claire. Then she added, "Ninety-two to go."

The girls dumped their trash in the large can near the doors that led to the playground and returned their trays to the stack. Honey slid her tray onto the highest stack, for a second the tower wobbled and Honey thought she'd be picking up trays for the entire recess but Claire steadied them just in time.

The early May sun warmed the playground, keeping the playground monitors in the shade next to the building. Honey scanned the playground. Jacob and Aiden were playing tetherball. On the soccer field, Walker scored another goal in a pick-up game.

"C'mon," Claire said. "Let's play soccer."

Honey wasn't good at soccer. "I'd rather swing."

"Yeah," Becky said. "I love to feel the wind in my hair."

"Why?" Claire asked.

Becky shrugged. "It makes me feel dramatic."

47

Honey liked Becky's flair for poetry and art. In a way it was like art was her destiny, like Harry's was magic. Honey did not have a great handle on what exactly destiny meant, at least not for her life. All she was ever really certain of was that her skin tingled and the hairs on her arms bristled whenever evil was near. And in Sleepy Hollow, she never had to go very far to feel it. But she also knew, like Harry, she had a part in helping to stop the evil from taking over completely. If that was her destiny, then that was fine with her.

"Come on!" Becky grabbed Honey's hand. "The swings are still open."

The girls ran to other side of the playground, but by the time they got there, only two empty swings were left. Someone would have to wait.

Claire shrugged. "I'd rather play soccer anyway."

48

Suddenly, Taylor darted between them and swiped one of the swings. "D'Shaunte," she yelled. "Now!"

Before Honey could move a muscle, D'Shaunte had her rear on the last swing. She grimaced at Becky. "Sorry. I have to obey them if I want to be in the club."

Honey felt a chill as the sun disappeared behind a cloud. Or maybe it was just the shadow of Clarice Kligore standing behind her.

"Sorry to get in your way again, Honey Moon. But I decided that my girls would have fun swinging." Clarice tossed her jet black hair over her shoulder. "If you want a turn, you can always join my club. You're so smart, I'd find you very useful."

Just like Mom found her useful for her chores? No, thank you.

"I will never join your numbskulled Royal Shades," Honey said. "I'd rather dance with Noah during gym class than let you boss me around."

"Really," Clarice said. "There are benefits to being a part of the club, as D'Shaunte is learning."

"And I'm her second-in-command." Taylor giggled as she pumped even higher on the swings.

Honey's skin tingled. This situation was making her angry. All she could do was watch Taylor and D'Shaunte pump their legs and swing higher and higher, laughing and cackling like ravens. How dare Clarice order one of her Shades to jump in front of her and take the swings. They knew she and Becky wanted

49

them. And how dare people step in front of her and walk slow just because they knew she was in a hurry. But as her anger grew, so did a plan. Clarice had Taylor bragging that she was her second-in-command. That meant Clarice was the boss. Honey wondered how many other kids, and maybe even teachers like Miss Fortissimo, Clarice was bossing around. Honey wouldn't be able to fight fire with fire on her own. She needed to recruit team members herself. Yep, that was the plan. Honey would form her own club.

She let the Shades swing. But this time, a smile burbled up from deep inside as Honey formulated her plan. Bullies would never take over her school.

The next day was Saturday. A day off. Well, mostly. Her mom still had a chore list but there was only one item on it. LAUNDRY. Harry had already washed Mom's van before running off with the DO NO EVIL Club.

51

"Laundry?" Honey said as she crumpled the paper into a ball and tossed it into the trash. "I hate laundry."

Honey buttered a slice of raisin toast. She could hear Mom in the living room with Harvest. Maybe the laundry could wait for a few minutes. She needed to find a place for her new club to meet. So, after wolfing down her toast, she ran out back where Dad was fussing with his car.

"I suppose I could make room in the garage for the lawn mower." Honey's dad ran a clean, white cloth along the length of the dipstick from his classic MG-F. "What did your mom say about her gardening tools?"

Honey sat on an overturned bucket and tapped her foot impatiently. "She said that if I organized the shed there'd be room enough for me and Becky and Claire to hang out in there. I have to ask her before I throw anything away, though."

"And you have to get your chores done before you can start working on the shed." With a swish, he settled the dipstick back into its slot. "What's behind you wanting a clubhouse all of a sudden? You girls haven't needed one before."

"The world is changing, Dad. We can't stay innocent, helpless children. It's time we take our place in the world and stand up for what is right."

Dad's eyes crinkled as he smiled. "That's how

it is, huh? This club is going to bring justice, order and goodness to Sleepy Hollow?"

"At least to the playground. I'll tackle the rest of the town later. I want to keep my expectations realistic."

"What's going on at the playground?" He reached under the hood to unscrew the cap of a tank. Then he pointed to a can of oil on the shelf behind Honey. Honey brought it to him, then stepped back as he broke the seal and poured the smelly liquid into a funnel he had placed in a pipe-thing inside the engine.

"There are some girls who are being real bullies. They think they are queens or something. Bossing everyone around. Even Brianna and she's so nice."

"Do the teachers know?"

"I told the music teacher they were walking slow in front of me, but she didn't even care." Which was an insult to the taxpayers of Sleepy Hollow. Weren't teachers supposed to

53

maintain order at school? Just think if everyone walked slow. The whole school would go crazy.

"If it were me, I'd rather walk slow than clean out that shed," Dad said. "Are you sure about this?"

Honey nodded. And she wouldn't say anything about Miss Fortissimo's threats. Her parents took her grades seriously. Almost as seriously as she did. She'd wait until she had more information before getting them involved with Miss Fortissimo, but the Royal Shades were fair game. "Yesterday they saw us on our way to the swings, so they jumped in front of us and wouldn't let us get on any swings."

"You're right. That's not very nice."

"And that's not all, Dad. I'm pretty sure they are recruiting, you know getting more mem-bers. Who knows how many Royal Shades there will be?"

"Royal Shades?"

54

"Yeah." Honey poked her head under the hood. "That's what they call themselves. Because they wear sunglasses."

"You know *shades* is another name for ghosts. Are these girls claiming to have some darker power?"

Her dad always came up with the best questions. "One of them said something about their sunglasses being magic, but I don't know if that's true. What could be the magic power? I haven't seen them do anything special be-sides strut around school like they are cool."

"Be careful." Dad pulled the oil can out of the funnel.

"I will, Dad. And, I think all that magic talk is silly. They just need to stop being so bossy— like they own the school."

Honey watched her father wipe his hands. "Remember, it's always easier to see when someone else is behaving badly than when you yourself are. What's the saying, *'Why do you notice the splinter in your brother's eye,* but you *ignore the log sticking out of your own eye?'* Watch yourself when you decide to correct someone else. Before you know it, you'll find that you are guilty of the same thing."

Her dad tossed the empty oil can into the dumpster. She ducked just in time. "Don't you worry. I'm not going to be mean. I'm going to fix this. People will be glad I'm taking control."

"Honey." Mom stuck her head out of the kitchen door. "Laundry. Now."

Dad smiled. "I'm sorry you got pushed around at school. Now it's your turn to push the buttons on the washer."

Honey rolled her eyes. "Very funny, Dad. Very funny."

∞

Honey looked at the washer. Mom said to put in the clothes. Add the soap. Turn this knob to wash and that was it. Sounded easy. She looked at the pile of clothes. It was mostly Harry's. Colorful tee shirts and boxers—white boxers.

"Mom said to separate it out. I guess she means to wash Harry's stuff alone and then do my clothes alone."

Honey dropped all of Harry's dirty clothes into the washer. Then she unscrewed the lid on a bottle of Ghost White Laundry Detergent. It smelled nice—like the backyard after a good rain. "Ohhh, now I sound like Becky."

She poured the blue liquid into the cap and dumped it into the washer tub. "Is that enough? Harry is pretty smelly." She poured another capful and then another and then another. "That should get rid of his nerdy stench."

57

Honey closed the lid, twisted the knob to wash, and heard the water begin to fill. She clapped her hands together. "That was easy. Nothing to do but wait. Probably an hour or two for all those clothes to get clean. Now to tackle the shed."

After a quick stop in the kitchen for a cookie, Honey texted Becky and Claire:

backyrd shed
now

Honey opened the shed door. It was pretty much filled to overflowing with yard work tools, the mower, about a thousand flower pots, bags of soil, and stinky fertilizer. She was glad Becky and Claire were on their way over to help. Honey had no trouble pulling the lawn mower out. She pushed it to the side. Next she lifted a lawn chair over two bags of Grow Well lawn seed and tossed it aside.

"How can two parents have so much stuff?"

"Hi, Honey." It was Becky riding onto the lawn, followed by Claire. Becky kicked her kickstand down, but it wouldn't hold her bike in the soft grass. She gave up and walked her purple bike to the side of the shed and propped it there.

"Hi," Honey said. "We got a lot of work to do."

"Why don't we just meet at Burger Heaven?" Claire asked. She wrinkled her nose at the dirty shed and dropped her bike with a thud. "This doesn't look like any fun."

Honey pulled another chair out of the shed and tossed it next to the other one. "It will be fun. But first we have to get our new clubhouse cleaned out. Then we'll put those Royal Shades in their place. We have to teach them that they can't go around telling us or anyone else what to do."

"I'm in," Claire blurted. "Did I tell you that they took the soccer ball after school yesterday and wouldn't let us play anymore. Aiden had to promise allegiance to Clarice before she'd give it back."

Promise allegiance? What kind of weirdo was she? Honey rubbed her knuckles. She would never, ever make any kind of deal with Clarice.

"Give me liberty or give me death," Honey said.

Claire laughed. "What's that supposed to mean?"

"I'm quoting one of our founding heroes. Just like Patrick Henry was standing against the tyrannical reign of King George, we've got to rebel against the Royal Shades and Clarice. We will not be bossed around by them. We are not their slaves. We are free!"

"Wow!" said Claire. "Best halftime locker room speech ever!" She held up her hand for a high-five. "Let's challenge them to an arm-wrestling match. Whoever is the strongest--"

60

"But what if they win?" Becky asked. "I'm not very strong. I can't ever do the flex-arm hang for long enough to win the Presidential Fitness Test."

"No arm wrestling," Honey said. "We're going to make our own club. We're going to out-think them." That was her strong suit, anyway.

"Yes!" Claire pumped her fist in the air. "Go team!"

But before they moved another muscle an ear-splitting cry came from Honey's house.

"What was that?" Honey asked.

"It came from your house," Becky said.

Honey looked for her dad but he and the car were gone. "Come on. Let's go."

The girls ran to the house. Honey pulled open the kitchen door just in time to hear her mother scream, "HONEY! WHAT HAVE YOU DONE?"

Honey froze. Becky froze. Claire said, "Uh oh!"

And then Honey saw it. A wave of soap bubbles near the laundry room door. "I wonder what happened."
"HONEY!"

"You better get in there," Becky said.

Honey stepped slowly into the laundry room where Mom stood ankle-deep in suds. Bubbles poured out of the machine.

"Soooo, what's up?" Honey said.

"I forget, five or six, maybe seven capfuls. Harry stinks, Mom."

Mom took a deep, deep breath. "All right. Get the mop. Clean this up. You'll have to scoop up the suds and dump them into the wash basin."

"We can help," called Becky.

Mom opened the lid and pulled out some wet, sudsy, heavy clothes. "Oh good grief, Honey Moon."

Honey grabbed the mop. "What now?"

"I told you to separate the clothes."

"I did. Mine and Harry's."

"That's not what I meant. Look what you did."

Mom held up two pairs of Harry's boxer shorts. "These used to be white. Now they're pink."

63

Honey swallowed a laugh.

"Harry will not appreciate pink shorts, Mom said.

Honey couldn't help it. A snicker escaped her mouth. "Sorry."

"You are supposed to separate the white clothes from the those colorful tee shirts."

"Oh," Honey said, shaking bubbles from her feet.

"Okay," Mom said. "I'm going to the market. Get this cleaned up."

Honey and Becky and even Claire did their best to clean up the mess. It didn't help that Half Moon wandered into the laundry and decided to roll around in the suds.

"This is impossible," she said. "I think we're fighting a losing battle."

"We just have to keep working," Becky said.

But before Honey could say another word another presence filled the room.

"Harry!" Honey said.

"Let me guess," he said. "Too much soap."

Honey smiled and said, "Help?"

Fortunately, Harry usually had a little magic for just that problem.

"Just a minute."

"What's he gonna do?" Claire asked.

Honey shrugged.

"This will do the trick—so to speak," Harry said. He dumped some bluish crystals onto the floor and in seconds the soap was absorbed into one medium sized pile which Honey was able to pick up and dump into the basin.

"Thanks, Harry," she said, doing her best to hide his now pink shorts.

65

"No problem," Harry said.

After snagging a couple of cookies, the girls went back to the shed. They still had a lot of work to do and none of them really felt like working. But Honey was determined.

"You should start with the small stuff, Claire," Honey said. "Some things like cracked flower pots and yucky dried leaves can go straight to the trash can."

"We should recycle this old bucket," Becky said. She held a beat up metal bucket with more dents than a golf ball.

"Good idea," Honey said. "Start a recycle pile over there."

"What's the name of the club?" asked Becky. "And will we have team colors? The Royal Shades wear those sunglasses all the time. Maybe we should all wear matching zebra print hair bows. That would be super cute."

Claire snorted. "As long as we don't have to carry matching turtle backpacks like Honey's."

Honey tried to ignore her. Ever since she got the baby looking turtle backpack at Christmas, she'd become a fifth-grade embarrassment. Funny thing was, as much as she hated carrying it, it did keep her company. She always felt like Turtle had her back, like Rabbit had Harry's. She rubbed her forehead. If she ever told anyone that, they'd think she was crazy for sure.

"Our first order of business is to clean out

the clubhouse." Honey said.

"Are we really gonna meet in here?" asked Claire.

"Sure," Honey said. "It'll be great."

Becky shook her head. "I don't know."

"C'mon, Becky, you love to decorate," Honey said.

"It doesn't need decorating," Becky said. "It needs decontaminating."

"Well, I'm going to help," Honey said. "As President I don't have to help, but since you and Becky just started your training I might as well lend a hand." Honey stepped toward the shed.

"Wait." Claire grabbed her by the shoulder. "What do you mean started our training?"

"You don't get to join the club without

doing something to earn it. And once you two are fully accepted members, then we'll let other people join and they will have to do the work. The more workers we have, the stronger we'll be."

"I don't mind helping," Becky said as she grabbed an old rag. "I'd feel bad asking other people to do my work for me."

"It's a great idea," Claire said. "We can jump in and get this old shed cleaned up, then everyone will want to join our club. Once we're the bosses, then it'll be the best club ever! We can just sit back and relax with cookies and milk."

Where did Claire get the idea that there'd be two bosses or three? Well, anyway, Honey wasn't going to argue. If they had more people join them than the Royal Shades had, she would consider her plan a success.

68

70

JUMP ROPE JINX

Abreeze ruffled Honey's plaid skirt as she walked past the statue of the Headless Horsemen on the square of Sleepy Hollow. Her skin prickled as usual. *Good old Sleepy Hollow.*

Sometimes she went the long way to school. That way she could avoid the Headless Horseman, but today she wanted to confront it head on. Or headless on, as the case may be.

So she stood facing the creepy statue. She had pulled herself up to full height. Why had Clarice decided to pick on her? Why was Miss Fortissimo doing their bidding? What did Paige mean when she said the glasses were magic? Did they give them special powers? Did she need to get something magical from Harry to compete?

Be brave, Honey Moon. Be brave.

It wasn't a voice Honey heard. Not really. More like an impression. She shrugged Turtle from her back and looked into its ugly face. "Did you say that?"

But just then, Taylor popped out from behind the statue and laughed. But Honey just shrugged her off also.

"You better listen to Clarice," Taylor said. "Or else!"

Honey pulled the turtle onto her back.

"Or else what?" Honey said. "She'll make me wear those stupid sunglasses?"

"Yeah." Taylor reached into her pocket and produced a pair of sunglasses. She propped them on her face. For a second or two she seemed to stare at Honey. But then, she took off like the Flash toward school.

Honey looked at the statue. "What's YOUR problem?"

The Horseman's collar stood up like a crown on his neck, while the face in his hands sneered at her. Why did Honey take these scary things so personally? Why couldn't she just ignore them? It was almost like they were challenging her to fight their darkness. And that's why she couldn't turn a blind eye when a group of shade-wearing girls started ruling over the fifth graders. She had to do something about it. Didn't everybody feel the same way?

73

I go where I am needed.

The eyes on the pumpkin head seemed to follow her as she passed. Her skin puckered up and the hair on the back of her neck prickled.

"It's just a statue," she told herself. "It can't do anything. I just have to get to school."

School. Who knew what kind of trouble waited for her there?

"Honey Moon."

Honey's heart dropped into her stomach. *Who said that?* She dared a glance back at the statue. The head's mouth still held the same snarl. But it sounded like it came from...

"I'm over here." Brianna waltzed out from behind a wide Maple tree. She was decked out in a long multi-layered coat and checkered hat. You never knew what to expect from Brianna.

"What are you dressed up for?" Honey asked.

"I'm listening to the adventures of Sherlock Holmes on audio book, so I decided to be him today."

That made sense. At least in the world of Brianna, it made sense.

Honey knew from her own reading that Sherlock Holmes was a master detective, so she asked, "What have you observed?" Honey ran her hand over her braid, feeling better now that Brianna was there. Someone who didn't mind standing up to the Royal Shades.

"I'm trying to solve the mystery of the Royal Shade sunglasses," Brianna said. She tapped her chin in a brainiac detective manner. "There are claims that they are magic."

Honey's hand tightened on the strap of her backpack. It was always a little embarrassing to admit you believed in magic, but Brianna didn't understand the concept of embarrassment.

"I heard that also, but I don't know how, or what kind of magic." Honey said as she started walking on the sidewalk toward school.

Brianna shrugged. "Let's look at the evidence." Honey expected her to pull out a magnifying glass and start inspecting things. "A couple members of the Royal Shades said that the glasses show them some secret information that is not obvious to the naked eye."

Honey nodded. "I heard Paige say something like that. At first I thought she was just trying to sound important. You know, pretending like they have powers that we don't know about, but that means Clarice shushed her."

"What exactly did she say?" Brianna asked.

"She said, the glasses help them see who is dangerous—at least I am pretty sure that was what she was gonna say before Clarice practically bit her head off."

She looked behind her again at the Scary One. "Oh, I shouldn't say that."

"Uhm." Brianna nodded and looked thoughtful.

"Clarice doesn't want anyone to know what the glasses do," Honey said. "And that's what makes me think that it is true. Clarice is the only dangerous one at the school. Maybe they can see what people are thinking."

"Not a chance," Brianna said. "If that were the case, they would've never left me alone with a pair of the glasses during gym class."

"You got their glasses?" Honey couldn't help but be impressed. People were always underestimating Brianna.

"Just for a few minutes while Paige was doing cartwheels, but what I saw was weird." Brianna paused as a squirrel stopped in their path. Its head moved in jerky motions, but Brianna stood still. Her eyes focused on the little animal.

Honey grabbed Brianna's arm and shook her. "Brianna? What was weird?"

Brianna spoke without switching her gaze from the squirrel. "Most everyone looked the same, but those who didn't were different. I ran over to the gym door and saw Miss Fortissimo walk past. She was tiny—smaller than a kindergartner. Mrs. Varsity had shoulders like a linebacker. She could've been a gladiator she was so big. That bully Jacob was barely bigger than the tennis ball he was holding. And Noah was as big as a grown-up."

"What good are sunglasses like that?" Honey asked. "Why would anyone want to see things all mixed up?"

"Then I saw a dark shadow cover over the gym. I smelled a hot smell, like burning leaves and heard a whooshing noise come from the door."

Honey's eyes widened. "What did you see? Who was it?"

"A threat. To them."

Honey swallowed. Her heart thumped hard.

"A threat? Like a . . . a creature or something? What did you see?"

"I saw you." Brianna seemed to look past Honey as she kept talking. "It was you, white hot, throwing hard shadows in every direction."

"Me?" Honey's mouth dropped open. "Me? I'm not a monster!" Honey could not believe her ears. "I don't understand."

Brianna shrugged.

"Tell me more," Honey said. "Is there more?" Honey's skin prickled worse than it had ever prickled.

Be brave, Honey Moon. Be brave.

"You were huge. And scary. You are their enemy. You don't look like everyone else to them."

"Why me? I'm not the bad guy."

"I didn't say you were bad—just scary,"

Brianna said, as if the world were really that simple. "There's something about you that threatens their plans. You have to be out of the way."

Honey did not like the sound of that. She looked at her phone. The early bell was about to ring, and she didn't dare arrive late again, but she had to know more. "How do you know this?"

Brianna didn't answer. She only looked to the sky.

"Ok," Honey said. "I . . . I know what I have to do."

"And what's that?" Brianna asked.

"Stop them."

The school loomed ahead. The raven, a huge black bird with a sharp hooked beak, glared at Honey from the school's sign out front. She never did like their mascot. It was so Sleepy Hollow, not cute and cuddly like Brighton Hill's bear mascot. The raven was a feathered menace that foretold doom.

"So they are coming after me?" Honey asked.

She looked for Brianna for an answer but she was gone.

Honey's stomach wobbled. The headless horseman was behind her and the raven was ahead of her. Threats all around her. As shocking as it was to hear herself described as a danger, something deep inside Honey rose to meet the description. They believed Honey was capable of disrupting their plans. She didn't know how she would do it, or what they were afraid of, but she did know she wasn't the type to give up. If Clarice Kligore and the Royal Shades thought she was coming after them, then maybe their glasses told the truth after all.

∽⌒∾

Honey watched her friend, Claire, on the sidelines of the gym, jumping up and down. Her ponytail bobbed as she swung her arms and sprung upward. "Got to get warmed up," she said. "Sitting at those desks is murder for muscle readiness and flexibility."

"We don't even know what game we're playing," Becky said.

"It doesn't matter." Claire reached up and tightened her ponytail holder. "I'll be at optimum performance ability in thirty seconds."

Honey stretched her arms too. It did feel good.

Mrs. Varsity blew her whistle and all the students dashed to the center of the gym and stood in a straight line.

"Today we're going to do a jump rope race," Mrs. Varsity called. She divided the students into teams. "Line up for the relay."

Jump rope races weren't Honey's favorite, but to be a well-rounded scholar, a true Renaissance woman, she needed to at least be competent in all subjects. Surely Marie Curie had mastered the jump rope race before she was awarded a Nobel prize for her work in radiation.

Naturally, Claire was at the front, waving frantically to Becky and her. "C'mon," she urged. "You too, Walker. We'll have the fastest team."

That was Claire, always looking for a competitive edge, even if it was something she thought sissy, like jumping rope. And if she didn't like the game they were supposed to play, she'd make up her own. Last year, before Mrs. Varsity could stop her, Claire had arranged for a jump rope gladiator match. Those beaded ropes left bruises. One demonstration and that game was banned forever and ever.

"I'll go first," Claire said. "To give us a lead. Honey, if you and Becky can hang in there, keep it tight, then Walker will run anchor. He should burn the competition away."

Walker looked at her with serious brown eyes. "I'm fast, but jumping rope while I run is going to slow me down."

Claire shrugged. "If you miss a few jumps, don't worry about it. Just keep running." She took the rope by the handles and narrowed her eyes at the far wall. "I'll be right back," she said. The other runners settled on the line too.

"Teams ready?" called Mrs. Varsity.

"Yes," they all sounded off.
"Ok, on my whistle."

The leaders took off and the gym erupted

in cheers as the racers ran their carefully measured steps. Noah, in the third line, had caught the rope around his ankle and stopped to untangle it. His team was nearly hoarse yelling at him.

Also yelling was the team next to Honey's team. "Go Royal Shades! Go Royal Shades! Lights out for everyone else!"

Honey's head snapped to face them. They clapped in time to Clarice's leading, their sunglasses sliding to the bridge of their noses.

"How did they all get on the same team?" she asked.

Becky shrugged. "They don't even have any boys."

Honey looked at Mrs. Varsity. She didn't seem to be paying much attention to what was happening in the race. "I bet Clarice has Mrs. Varsity in her clutches too."

"But they aren't winning," Becky said. As

promised, Claire led all the other teams. She ran like a machine, rope clicking against the gym floor in a perfect rhythm. She reached the boundary line at the end of the room and spun to return. A quick scan of her competition, only now passing half court and she nodded in satisfaction. Time for the quick run back.

"No," Honey said. "Watch out, Claire!"

Whack! Taylor stumbled just as she was meeting Claire on her way back. Taylor's jump rope snaked around Claire's foot, then with a mighty yank, she jerked it back, pulling Claire's feet off the ground and landing her smack dab on her chin.

"Ooooo...." The class moaned in unison.

Claire was stunned. She laid there flat on the ground. Taylor picked up her jump rope, raced to the wall, turned and was coming back by. Her sunglasses hadn't even moved.

"Get up!" Honey yelled. "Get up!"

Becky's hand covered her mouth. "Do you think she's hurt?"

"It doesn't matter," Honey said. "She wants to win. Get up!"

Honey looked for the teacher but she had her back turned, talking with another student.

Claire stood. She was a little wobbly, but determined. Blood trickled down her chin and onto her neck. She would finish the race, but she couldn't catch Taylor. It would be up to the rest of them. Honey winced to see the blood dribbling from Claire's chin. When Claire reached the finish line she handed Becky the rope.

87

"You might need a stitch in that," Becky said.

"Go!" said Claire. "You're wasting time."

Becky bit her lip, then started her leg of the race.

"Cool!" Walker said. "That could leave a scar."

Claire grabbed Honey by the shoulders. "She did that on purpose. Did you see it? She did it on purpose." A drop of blood fell from her chin and splattered on the floor. "We have to beat them."

Becky was catching up with D'Shaunte. The Shades cheered as they approached the line for the next leg. Honey toed the line. There might be other teams racing, but all they cared about were the two at the far end of the gym.

Becky huffed to the line and held out the rope to Honey. Honey couldn't let her team down. She had to win this for them.

She got off to a slow start. The handles were twisted and then, when she got them into her hands the right way, the rope had twined around her arm. But she shook it loose. She could do this. She could win. She had to beat the Shades.

Honey would have to hurry to catch Clarice. Clarice had a head start, but Honey was finding her stride. Click, step, click, step, click, step... Honey wasn't the fastest, but she was consistent.

The gap was closing. "Come on, Honey," she whispered. "Concentrate. Don't miss a step. No mistakes and you can do this. You can beat the Royal Pains."

Honey closed the gap. She was about to catch Clarice, but somehow she was getting off track. She was getting closer and closer to Clarice. No, it wasn't Honey's fault. Clarice was swerving into Honey's lane, leaving Honey no room to get around her. Honey angled toward the wall, but Clarice kept going at a diagonal, pushing Honey closer and closer to the bricks. Honey's blood boiled. She looked at the sidelines. Claire was jumping and waving her arms, trying to get Mrs. Varsity's attention while Taylor was cheering Clarice even further into Honey's lane. But again Mrs. Varsity was distracted. Honey tried to focus back on the race.

Honey would not be squeezed out. Enough was enough. She lowered her jump rope, and with the next swing, caught Clarice's jump rope and pinned it beneath her foot. Clarice skidded to a stop. Her black hair flew as she spun around. She was probably glaring, but from behind the sunglasses, Honey couldn't be sure.

"Get off my rope." Her blood red mouth was a tight line.

"Get out of my lane," Honey said. The other teams were catching them, and Honey didn't even care. Clarice yanked on the rope, but Honey just ground her foot down harder. "I'm not letting go until you learn to stay where you belong."

Then all of a sudden Mrs. Varsity towered over them. "What are you doing, Honey?"

Clarice answered. "I was winning, so she grabbed my rope. She's trying to make us lose, Mrs. Varsity. Honey Moon is a big, fat baby."

Honey gasped. "What?"

"That's right," Taylor called and the whole line of Royal Shades nodded their heads as innocent as angels.

"I don't doubt it," Mrs. Varsity said. "Honey has a bad habit of winning at any cost." Her eyes grew big as she spotted Claire. "And what happened to your chin?"

Claire brushed away another drop of blood, leaving it smeared on her face. "Taylor tackled me. She fell and hit my foot..."

"She just happened to fall down," Mrs. Varsity said, "and just happened to hit your foot? Sounds like Claire tripped her, then kicked her when she was down. I should've never let you two on the same team."

Honey watched as Mrs. Varsity looked at Clarice and smiled. A chill like a thousands creepy, crawly ants ran down her spine.

"How about me?" Walker asked. "I never even got to race."

"The whole team is disqualified," Mrs. Varsity said. "I will not tolerate cheating or violence."

"They were in our lane," but Honey's protests were drowned out by the squealing cheers of the Royal Shades.

"We won, we won," they chanted.

Honey walked back to Claire dragging the jump rope behind her.

"How do they think they won?" Becky asked.

"They didn't even finish the race and there were other teams that did."

"They won because they kept us from winning," Honey said. "And they got us in trouble. That was their goal."

"It's not fair," Becky said. "And Mrs. Varsity just let them—"

"Take over," Honey said. "Just like Miss Fortissimo."

93

Becky shook her head. "I . . . I almost feel like crying."

"Don't," Honey said. "They haven't met our club yet. But when they do, they'll be sorry."

94

HONEY'S BEES

The washing machine fiasco took so long to clean up that Honey and her friends did not have time to finish cleaning out the shed that very sudsy day. So they made plans to work on it again after school. But only after Honey wrapped up her chores. Her list included vacuuming and dusting. She finished both tasks as fast as she could while Becky and Claire waited outside.

"It's even more important that we get our club up and running," Honey said when she joined them. "Especially now after what they did in PE."

Sweat ran down Honey's back as she dragged out the last of the patio chairs. The shed had felt crowded when they'd started cleaning it, but now it seemed as big as the gymnasium at school. Just when she thought they were making progress, Honey would spot another stack of flower pots, another uncoiled garden hose, another broken bag of cedar chips spilling out on the floor. How did the small, square building hold so much stuff?

But once it was aired out, they'd be fine. It'd be the perfect place to plan a counterattack on the Royal Shades.

"We still haven't decided on a name for our club," Claire said. "How about the Celtics?"

"No," Becky said. "We are not a basketball team."

Honey waved a rake at the corner to snatch at the spider webs. "Well, they are calling themselves royal. We should think of something that is just as royal, maybe even more royal."

"Princesses!" Becky smiled despite her watery eyes. "What goes with Princesses? Pretty Princesses? Perfect Princesses?"

"Ewww!" Claire leaned on a shovel. "I get so sick of all the princess stuff."

But Becky was on a roll spewing out ideas about how they could princess the place up. "We'll paint those terra cotta flower pots pink and yellow, then we'll hang them across the ceiling. Oh.... even better. I could string Christmas lights through the holes in the bottom of the pots. They'll scatter the light into whatever colors we choose. And then--"

"Not pink and yellow," Honey blurted. "That doesn't look very tough."

Becky frowned. "Are we supposed to be tough? I thought this was going to be fun."

97

What was more fun than being tough? "But we have to put the Royal Shades in their place. And to do that, we got to be tough . . . and brave."

Becky wiped dirt from her blue leggings. "I know but . . . but I don't want to fight."

"Don't worry," Honey said. "There's different ways to fight."

98

Claire made a fist and slammed it into her palm. "I'm ready. Just in case." Then she lightly touched the butterfly closure on her chin.

"How about yellow and black?" Honey asked. "That's a compromise. The yellow is energizing and the black lets people know not to mess with us."

Claire smiled. "That's the Pittsburgh Steelers' colors so it's okie dokie with me."

"But yellow and black aren't really princess colors," Becky said.

"Thank goodness," said Claire.

"We don't have to be princesses," Honey said. "What can be *better* than princesses?" She scratched her chin and thought, even though she already had a name in mind all along. "I've got an idea. How about The Queen Bees?"

Claire's eyes darted to the open garage door. "Would that have something to do with a yellow and black bicycle in that garage that happens to have a license plate on it that reads HONEYBEE?"

"Honey bees, queen bees, I suppose there's a connection," Honey said. "But the honey bee is one of the most beneficial animals in nature. Honey bees are not only responsible for all the world's honey supply, but they also pollinate hundreds of different fruits, vegetables and flowers. The honey bee works tirelessly and unselfishly. She--"

"We get it," Claire responded. "I'm not asking for a three-page report on honey bees. All we need is a name. That's all."

"I guess Queen Bees sounds okay," Becky said just before she let go a loud sneeze that echoed inside the metal shed.

Claire laughed. "Now that didn't sound very princess-like."

"So, it's settled," Honey said, feeling very satisfied.

Claire took up a push broom and swung it like a sword. "When are we going to let more people join our group?"

"First we need to make the rules and figure out what they need to do to join," Honey said.

Becky sorted through the plastic flower pots tossing the cracked ones into the trash bin they'd pulled out of the garage. "We can have a secret handshake and a song. And we'll each have a Secret Sis. That's where you draw names and then you give your Secret Sis gifts and write her encouraging notes. My mom's sorority does it."

"There are only three of us," Claire said. "I don't think it would be very secret."

"Then we can wait until more people join," Becky said. "But it's a sweet idea. It'll build bonding and sisterhood."

Honey was seriously afraid that Becky had the wrong idea. Somehow she had a vision of a weekly tea party no matter how many times she told her that the goal of the club was to stand against the Shades. Honey was more interested in finding troops to command. But Becky was might be on to something. If she listened to Becky, she'd probably get more recruits. Becky had good ideas when it came to girl stuff.

By the time they got the shed emptied, the sun was sinking behind the rooftops.

"I'm still confused about something," Claire said. "What exactly are we going to do—the Queen Bees, I mean. How are we going to take down the Shades?"

"Yeah," Becky said. "Just what will we do?"

Honey was quiet a moment. She was remembering what Brianna told her about how she was dangerous to the Shades. "We're going to . . . to stand up against them. I will tell everyone who joins what to do and what to say to them. We will refuse to follow them."

"What are we going to do with all this stuff?" Claire asked.

102

"Most of it can stay outside," Honey said. "But my dad's mower will have to go back inside the shed."

"I'm going to take these old pots," said Becky. "I'll bring them back, ready to be installed."

Honey nodded. This was working out perfectly.

EXTREME CLUBHOUSE MAKEOVER

At breakfast the next morning, Honey was working on a bowl of Chocolate Skulls when Mom reminded her about chores. Honey's heart sank. "Mom," Honey said. "I will be happy to do these chores but I was hoping I could have just today off. I have important club plans and . . . and—"

"Honey," Mom said as she pushed a sippy cup into Harvest's diaper bag. "I think I know what you're going to say. But no. Chores come first."

Honey zipped up her turtle backpack. She would be on time today—even if she took the long way to avoid the Headless Horseman.

"Bye, Mom. Bye, Harvest."

"Don't forget, Honey," Mom said. "Chores first."

"The injustice of it all," Honey said. Then she bolted through the back door to school.

The school day pretty much went off without a hitch or a major Royal Shade disturbance. But this only made Honey even more concerned. They could be planning something big. But she was happy for a peaceful day. Even though she did notice more kids wearing those same sunglasses.

I need to stop them.

The Queen Bees met at Becky's house because it would take all three of them to carry the decorations back to the clubhouse. Becky had been busy cutting and gluing and stringing and creating. It was Claire's job to bring the snacks.

Becky led the way to her magical craft room. Being the only child of two artistic types, Becky's spare room had been transformed into a creative wonderland. Every kind of paint, pencil, canvas, ribbon, glitter and bead was neatly organized and available to produce masterpiece after masterpiece. And Becky did.

What had formerly been ordinary terra cotta flower pots were now painted black and yellow. They stretched out on the countertop that ran along the length of the room and were all attached by an electrical cord.

"I like the colors," Honey said.

"Thank you," Becky said. "My dad had to help with the wiring but they turned out real nice. Look." Becky took the end of the cord and plugged it into the outlet. Immediately the pots lit up and the lights inside streamed out. Every other pot had a yellow light bulb so the light looked striped.

"Awesome!" Claire said.

"And here are a few posters I made." Becky held up a yellow poster board with big, black and silver striped letters.

QUEEN BEES

WE BRING THE SWEET ...
AND THE STING!

The other poster had a cute honeybee on it wearing a crown.

"Nice," Honey said.

"Well it took some work, but I think it'll give that old shed a better sense of atmosphere,"

Becky said.

"Yeah," Claire said. "You're the Mickey Mantle of the craft world."

Honey looked at Claire. "Did you get the snacks?"

"Cookies and juice boxes. Mom has them ready."

"Let's go," Honey said. "We can walk by your house on the way."

107

Figuring out how to carry Becky's flower pot lights took some time, though. Before, the flower pots stacked neatly inside each other, but now with light bulbs inside each one, they were not only breakable, but awkward to carry. Finally, they laid them in a wicker picnic basket Mrs. Young said they could borrow. Honey and Becky walked down the sidewalk, each holding a handle, while Claire ran ahead to get the snacks. The posters were rolled up under their arms.

The basket handles weren't comfortable. It wasn't that the basket was too heavy, but the wicker dug into Honey's hand. Two houses down from Claire's, she finally spoke up.

"Can we put this down for a minute? I want to get a better grip."

"Sure." Becky rubbed her hand against her shorts. "I could use the break too." Then she noticed the overgrown yard they'd stopped in front of. "Look at all those weeds," Becky said. "It's a pity. There are a lot of nice flowers in the flower beds, but no one will see them if they don't mow."

Everyone else's yard looked nice. What was the story here? Just then the door opened and a very familiar face appeared.

"I thought that was you, Honey." Mrs. Wilcox, Harvest's nanny, stepped outside.

"Hey," Honey said. "You said you couldn't watch Harvest because your mom was sick. What are you doing here?" Finally, the tables had turned. Mrs. Wilcox tattled on Honey all the time. She couldn't expect any mercy when she was caught breaking the rules.

Mrs. Wilcox put her hand on her hip. "This is my mother's house, Honey Moon. The one who's sick. That's why I'm here. Better luck next time."

"Oh." Honey looked away. She had a kind of bad habit of jumping to wrong conclusions.

"Your mother is sick?" Claire asked. "Is that why the yard is such a mess?"

Mrs. Wilcox cringed. "I'm going to mow it as soon as I get back from the pharmacy."

"It's not that bad." Becky was always making people feel nice.

Mrs. Wilcox smiled. "Thank you, dear. I can handle the mowing but those flowerbeds, well, they'll just have to wait. I've told Mother that she has too many, but she loves them. Hopefully she'll be back on her feet soon and can enjoy some of this nice sunshine." She motioned to the basket. "Speaking of flowers, what have you got there, girls?"

Mrs. Wilcox might not be babysitting today, but she was still in nanny mode.

"We cleaned out that shed in the backyard," Honey said. "Mom was going to throw away these pots, but we've decorated them instead."

"And turned them into lights," Becky added.

"Excellent idea," Mrs. Wilcox said. "Then I won't keep you. Thank your mother for giving me this time off. Tell her that I don't know when I'll be back, but I want to keep watching Harvest just as soon as I'm able."

Poor woman. How bad must her mother be if she'd rather babysit Harvest? Honey bent to pick up her handle, but Becky only stood there looking at the house.

"I feel guilty, Honey. Here we are decorating flower pots for a garden shed, when Mrs. Wilcox's mother needs her yard work done. Doesn't that seem silly?"

111

Oh no. Becky, who would take in every stray animal she saw, was now going to adopt yards and flowerbeds?

"We can't do everything for everyone," Honey said. "Besides, you see what's been happening at school. We have to stand up to the Royal Shades. Mrs. Wilcox can take care of this. We have to follow our own destiny."

Destiny. Was it their destiny to stand up to the Shades?

Just go where you are needed.

Honey shook her head. Honey's destiny did not involve doing other people's chores. She had to fight fire with fire. And speaking of chores. Honey was ditching hers and she just had a worry thought that Mrs. Wilcox might tell her mom. But she shook that terrible thought from her head.

"Let's go," Honey said. "Grab the basket. Claire's probably waiting for us."

112

Honey and Becky lugged the basket to Claire's house. They set it down again and waited for Claire, who appeared with a brown paper grocery bag. She looked straight at Honey and then at Becky.

"What's wrong? You two look like you saw a ghost or Old Pumpkin-head came to life."

"Nothing that exciting," Honey said. "Just an overgrown lawn."

"What?" Claire said.

"Your neighbor's house. Mrs. Wilcox's mother could use some help that's all."

"Oh, yeah. Her yard is a mess."

"And we could help," Becky said.

"No," Honey said. "Let Harry's DO NO EVIL club do it. We have bigger fish to fry."

Honey had her hands full organizing the Queen Bees. She couldn't take on a city beautification project right now. Especially in Sleepy Hollow where every street light was decorated with ghoulish creatures, trash cans were shaped like tombstones, and pretty flower arrangements were decked with spider webs just so they didn't look too happy. First, they had to deal with the Royal Shades.

Honey and Becky hauled the basket the rest of the way to the Moon's home, with Claire munching on cookies the entire way. Her hand was plunged deep into the bag as they reached the gate. Honey rattled the gate to make sure her dog, Half Moon, wasn't loose in the yard before opening it. The coast was clear.

Honey slid the clubhouse door open.

"Let's get the lights up first," Becky said. "That will make the room feel more homey. I saw a stepladder in there."

Honey nodded. "I'll help you while Claire gets the snacks ready."

114

"You want to eat already?" Claire wiped a smeared chocolate chip off her mouth. "I'm not hungry."

Of course she wasn't hungry. She'd already eaten half the cookies.

"Then set up the chairs," Honey said. "There's a mud mat on the bottom shelf. Put it beneath the chair in the center and then put your chairs on either side." That would look just fine, like the long carpets that lead up to a queen's throne in the throne room. And she'd have Becky and Claire as her ladies in waiting. And later there'd be more.

Honey unfolded the stepladder and held out her hand for the zip-ties to hang the string of lights and flower pots. Becky reached up with a zip-tie and balanced on a chair that Claire put out.

"So once we get this ready," Honey said. "Who else do we want to invite?"

"That depends," Claire said. "What do they have to do for us?"

"Claire," said Becky. "We don't want to be bossy."

Claire rolled her eyes. Honey had to tread carefully. "We aren't going to be bossy, but being in the Queen Bees is an honor. And it's an honor they have to earn. We can't just let everyone show up and call themselves a part of our club. That would get out of control." And Honey was all about control.

"Emily would be a good addition," Claire said. "She's on my softball team and she would be good in a fight."

"We aren't going to fight," Becky said.

"Did you see what they did to me?" Claire lifted her chin and pointed at the band-aid. "We have to defend ourselves."

Becky shook her head. "I was thinking more of Brianna. She might want to join. She sure doesn't let Clarice tell her what to do."

Brianna didn't let anyone tell her what to do, or at least she pretended not to hear most of the time. Sometimes she got to go to special classes, sometimes she left pages of her homework blank, and sometimes she knew answers no one else knew. She might not follow directions very well, but Honey was always fascinated by the things she came up with.

"Brianna, definitely," said Honey. "We'll invite her just as soon as you both finish your probation."

"Probation? What does that mean?" Claire set a chair down with a thud that raised a cloud of dirt from the mat.

"It means that you aren't full members yet," Honey said. "You are still trying out. You have to earn your membership and since we just got started, there hasn't been time for you to do all that you need to do."

"I can't believe this--"

"Oh, Claire," said Becky. "It's not bad. I'm having fun decorating the clubhouse. It looks great."

117

"And you didn't make those cookies anyway," Honey said.

"Well, my mom did, and if it weren't for this club, I could've kept them and ate them all myself."

"And if it weren't for this club, you could try to fight the Royal Shades all by yourself," Honey said.

"We're not fighting," Becky repeated. She hopped down from the stepladder and grabbed the end of the extension cord. "You two behave yourselves while I plug this in."

"Go for it," Honey responded.

With a little grunt Becky plugged the cord into the extension cord that stretched from the garage and the little room was suddenly dancing in beams of yellow light. In that moment the place went from dingy garden shed to pretty clubhouse. The girls stood in amazement, heads tilted back, mouths hanging open at the dear little lanterns Becky had fashioned. They transformed the dreary shed into a magical area fit for any queen.

"This is going to be awesome," Honey said. The light fell on the three chairs, lighting them up like they were props on a Broadway stage. She could just imagine herself sitting on the lawn chair throne in her beautiful pink and gray dress from the Valentine's Dance.

"Let's get the posters up," Becky said. "When the light catches the glitter--"

"Honey?" It was her mom, ducking her head to step into the small space. "Wow, girls. You have done a fabulous job in here." She turned a full circle slowly, like she did when she first walked into a nice hotel room. "I'm impressed with all the work you've done."

They had worked hard--Becky more than anyone--but that didn't stop Honey from basking in her mother's praise. Honey wasn't much on decorating. She was more likely to rearrange participles in English and exponents in math than her bedroom furniture, but she appreciated the transformation they'd accomplished in the otherwise crowded space.

119

"Wait until we get the posters hung," Honey said.

"I hate to interrupt your fun," Mom said. "But Honey hasn't done her chores yet."

"Chores?" Honey covered her eyes. "You've got to be kidding. Now? But, Mom. We have so much to do."

"I'm not kidding. Come on in. It won't take you too long."

"Becky and Claire can help me. They are trying out for the Queen Bees and are still on probation. They'll do whatever I tell them."

Her mother's chin jutted out and her eyes narrowed. "Excuse me? You think I'm going to let them do your chores? That's not happening."

"We'll wait on you." Claire dropped into a chair—the center chair, the one on the carpet—and rattled her bag of cookies. "Becky and me can eat cookies until you get back."

"What?" Honey held her hands out. "That's not right. I'm the leader. I should get more cookies than anyone."

"Honey Moon," Mom said. "That is an awful attitude. You get inside right now. Don't you worry about what your friends are doing."

Impossible. This chore thing needed to come to a sudden and brutal end. People like Honey didn't have time to do chores. They were too important. They had bigger issues to worry about.

120

Honey stomped through the back door and marched to the refrigerator. The first thing she saw was the Anisha from India letter. All she wanted was to learn how to read and have a new pencil she could keep sharp. What it must be like to only have those small things to worry about? Honey had school, the Queen Bees, the Royal Shades, and her infernal chores to worry about.

Beneath Anisha's profile page, under the New York magnet, was the chore chart. Honey had earned a star for every day until today. And today's chore read: Give Half Moon his bath.

Honey ripped the page off the fridge. She could almost feel steam coming out her ears. "Do you see what this says? Wash the dog? Isn't Half Moon more Harry's dog than mine?"

"Harry isn't going to be home until late tonight. I'm fixing supper and I've had Harvest all day. Until Mrs. Wilcox's mother gets better, you've got to help out more. And today that means washing the dog."

How humiliating. The leader of the revolution shampooing a big, floppy-eared mutt. Honey just bet that Joan of Arc didn't have to bathe animals. She probably had the captured English soldiers do it for her. But Honey had to do what she had to do.

She grabbed Half Moon's leash. Why did dogs need baths, anyway? It seemed like an animal should be allowed to smell like an animal. She didn't want the other dogs to make fun of Half for smelling like a strawberry pop-tart. Harry smells like Harry doesn't he? Honey couldn't help but laugh at her own joke.

"Half Moon," she called. "Come here, boy."

Half came bounding into the kitchen. Honey grabbed his collar and attached the leash.

The dog jumped up and down. He snatched the leash midway between his teeth and tried to rip it out of her hands. "Stop it," Honey said. "We're not going on a walk. Calm down."

Naturally Half didn't understand her. She

122

grabbed the shampoo and brush her mother had set out on the kitchen counter and led Half Moon outside. He jumped and barked and wagged his tail. "I said calm down. No walk. A bath." Honey looped the leash around the leg of the grill and hooked up the water hose.

Now Half really got excited. He crouched down with his rear in the air and his tail wagging. Honey caught the leash in one hand and tried to hold him still while squirting him with water. Half thought it was a game. He twirled around snapping his jaws trying to catch the stream. While she was soaking down Half Moon, Honey looked toward the shed.

Becky and Claire waved. Honey was pretty sure she heard them laughing.

"Stop it, Half," Honey ordered. "Stop!" The last thing she wanted was to look like a fool in front of her new acolytes. Acolytes--a word meaning a *person who admires and faithfully follows a leader.* That's what Honey needed. Some faithful followers who would take care of these messy chores and let her rule in peace. Queen Bees weren't supposed to smell like wet dog.

Half's fur turned dark and slick with the water. Honey set the hose down and grabbed the shampoo bottle. Pink soap bubbled through the clear container, and oozed out as she squeezed. Tossing the shampoo container aside, Honey ruffled Half's fur, being sure to scrub all the way to his skin, just like Harry had taught her. Where was Harry? This was his dog. Shouldn't he be the one doing the dirty work?

Acolytes. Harry had them and she didn't. But that was changing.

Having scrubbed Half every inch from his floppy ears to his waging tail, Honey picked up the water hose and squashed her thumb over the opening to spray with more accuracy and force. She started at Half's head so she could get the soap out and work her way down, but Half didn't enjoy being squirted in the face. He jerked backwards. The grill screeched across the concrete patio.

124

"Stop it, Half," Honey ordered. She grabbed the grill by the leg to keep it from toppling, but Half hadn't given up. Jerking like a trout on a hook, he yanked his head out of his collar and took off at a full run. Suds flew behind him as he streaked around the yard.

125

"This isn't a game," she hollered. Half's tail wagged like crazy. His pink tongue waved in his breeze of hot, doggy breath as he panted happily. "Come back here."

But instead he took off. Straight for the clubhouse.

Becky and Claire had already gone back inside, and when Half tore into the building, their screams filled the yard.

"Wet dog!" Becky yelled. "Wet dog on my posters."

"Stop eating the cookies," Claire hollered. "Bad dog! Bad dog!"

Honey raced to the clubhouse. Half ran figure eights through the lawn chairs. Muddy footprints stamped across Becky's carefully designed posters. Becky grabbed one by the corner and tugged it out from under Half. Half lost his balance and fell on his side, leaving a body-sized print of a wet dog smack-dab in the middle of the queen bee.

Half scrambled to his feet. Honey scrambled to her throne. "Stand in front of the door," she said. "We'll trap him."

Half cocked his head at their slow approach. Maybe he was tired of the chase. Whatever the reason, he didn't run again. He just waited until they were nearly within arms' reach, and then he made that uniquely doggy move that shakes off all the excess water in a canine coat, only in this case, that water came accompanied by large clumps of glitter.

Splashes of glitter stuck against every wall, chair, rug and decoration. Even the flower pot lights weren't spared.

"How are you going to beat the Royal Shades," Claire asked, "when you can't even control your dog?"

Acolytes—they weren't always what you hoped.

128

THE BUBBLE BEAST

The Queen Bees had a plan. It took a day of remaking posters and cleaning the clubhouse again, but finally with their home base completed, the Queen Bees were ready to sting. And sting they would.

The cafeteria smelled pretty much the way it always did. The aroma of the warm, yeasty rolls made their stomachs growl, although the actual taste was usually disappointing. Honey's plastic lunch tray bumped into Claire's as she slid it along the metal tracks toward the lunch ladies.

"One scoop of green beans, three chicken nuggets, and a roll. Be sure and clean your plate." The hair-netted lunch lady dropped the roll and repeated her mantra with Honey, but Honey was in a hurry and nearly took out before the roll was safely in its spot.

"Let's go, let's go," she said. "We've got to eat and get out there."

So the Royal Shades thought she looked scary? Well, today she was going to live up to her reputation.

Claire had already crammed her roll into her mouth before they reached the table. Becky tossed her milk carton into the trash as she jogged to reach them. "No time for a drink," she said, and slid into her seat. One nugget disappeared with her next breath.

"Can I sit with you?" It was Brianna, wearing a velvet Little Red Riding Hood cape and tall boots.

"Sure," Becky said. "But we're in a hurry."

Brianna swept her cape aside as she took a seat. "Where are you going?"

"We're going outside," Claire said. "We're going to get on the swings first and beat the Royal Shades."

131

Brianna lowered her eyes. "Do you want to swing that badly?"

"We have to swing," Honey said. "Because they won't let us." Sometimes you had to prove a point, even if the issue wasn't that important to you.

"So you don't want to swing, but you're going to because the Royal Shades want you to?"

"No, we're doing it because they don't want us to," Claire said. "That's why it's fun."

Brianna speared a green bean and chewed it thoughtfully. "It doesn't make sense to me."

Which wasn't surprising. Brianna specialized in knowing what no one else could figure out. But something as simple as revenge was incomprehensible to her.

132

"Brianna, would you like to join our club?" Becky asked. "We're called the Queen Bees. We have a clubhouse with lights that are striped like a honey bee and snacks. It's really cool."

Brianna smiled.

"Please," Honey said. "We'd love to have you."

"I'll think about it," Brianna said. "Are you late for swinging?"

Honey's jaw tightened. She scanned the cafeteria. Some of the kids from the first class in line were standing up, collecting their trash.

"Time to go," she said. The three girls jumped to their feet.

"Bye, Brianna," Becky called as they raced out the doors.

The playground was empty. Perfect. Their plan was working.

"Hooray!" Honey shouted. "We're first." The three girls ran to the swings and threw themselves into them. Flying through the air, Honey had never felt more free. She looked at Becky, whose long, brown curls were streaming behind her, and smiled.

133

Claire straightened her arms and leaned all the way back until her head nearly brushed the ground as she swooped down, and then back up. "Woo-hoo!" she cheered.

But as their victory shouts grew louder, Honey noticed that there was an empty swing. She bit her lip. Couldn't have even one Royal Shade get it. That would ruin their campaign. But how could they save it? The cafeteria doors opened and a group of boys streamed out. They ran straight for the ball bin and grabbed the soccer ball, rushing to get a few minutes of their game done before the whistle was blown. They wouldn't help. Maybe Brianna would come out, but instead Honey spied Paisley.

Paisley was tall, thin, and as graceful as a ballerina, because she was a ballerina. She was also good at races and sit-up contests. Of course she could do the splits, so no one had splits contests with her anymore.

"Paisley," called Honey. "Do you want to swing with us?"

Paisley ran a hand over the heavy twist of hair on the top of her head. She'd make a perfect Queen Bee. Her braided bun already looked like a tiara. "Sure, I guess." Paisley took the final swing and soon was flying with the rest of them.

"So, here's the deal," Honey said. "We're starting a new club, the Queen Bees. Do you

134

want to be in it?"

Paisley grinned. "I guess so."

"Great. We meet at my house after school, because that's where our clubhouse is. Once you do a few weeks of service, then you're a full member, just like Claire and Becky."

"A few weeks?" Paisley said. "That seems like a long time."

"Yeah, Honey," Becky said. "We didn't have to serve that long."

"Okay, fine. Then just for this week. After that you are a full member."

"And what do we do?" Paisley asked.

"Mostly we frustrate the Royal Shades," Claire said as she whooshed down between them.

"Isn't that Clarice Kligore's group?" Paisley said. "I'm sick of them. They told me I couldn't go the bathroom in the downstairs girls' room because they were using it. I had to go all the way to one near the office. Then I got into trouble for missing so much class."

"That's awful," Becky said.

"What I don't get is why the Royal Shades are allowed out of class so much? Some of the teachers seem to be . . . to be—"

"One of them?" Honey said.

"Yes. It's creepy. But then again, this is Sleepy Hollow."

"They won't do that to you again," Honey said. "Not if we stick together."

"And can I invite Madeline?" Paisley asked.

Then they would be up to five. The shed might not be big enough for their meetings. But that was okay. Some Queen Bees could sit outside. "Sure," Honey said with a smile. The pieces were falling into place.

The girls continued to swing. Pumping so hard and soaring so high that they got the bumps. Claire laughed. Honey laughed, but Becky said the bumps made her scared.

"Speaking of scared," Honey said. "Look over there."

It was Clarice, Taylor, D'Shaunte and Paige. They were standing near the basketball hoop and looking right at the swings--at least Honey thought they were looking at them. It was hard to tell through those dark glasses. But they were certainly pointed in their direction.

"They see us," Claire hooted. The toes of her tennis shoes pointed straight up like she was going to kick the sun.

"Look happy," Honey said, but she didn't need to remind them. Nothing could make her happier than seeing Clarice standing like a statue with no swing to swing on. Victory was hers. But then Honey's skin prickled.

Stay the course, Honey Moon. Stay the course.

The Shades spun around in a tight, mean little maneuver and stormed back inside.

"Where are they going?" asked Claire.

"Probably to tattle on us," said Becky.

"We aren't doing anything wrong," Honey said. "Just swinging."

Soon the Royal Shades were back. Clarice was holding a small duffle bag. From the way she strutted you'd think it was full of gold. With her followers behind her, she strolled to the four-square court and dropped it to the ground. Pointing her finger, she directed Taylor to bend down and open it. She did have command of her troops. Honey had to respect her for that. Taylor pulled out a large, colorful wand and showed it to the kids gathered around while D'Shaunte unscrewed the lid off a big plastic bottle and poured a shimmery liquid into a flat pan.

Paisley had nearly stopped swinging. "What is it?" she asked.

Clarice took a wand from the bag and dipped it into the flat pan. A crowd of kids had gathered around her, making it hard to see what was happening in the middle. Only when Honey swung high could she see Clarice waving the wand. Suddenly, the circle of kids jumped back with squeals of delight as a multicolored bubble floated above their heads.

"Bubbles?" Claire said. "They got the bubbles from the supply closet. How lame."

139

But there was something different about this bubble. It looked stronger and brighter than any bubble Honey had ever seen before. The colors were real, not just floaty hints of rainbow. And it wasn't round. It bent and moved like it had a life of its own. In fact, as Honey watched, it took a very un-bubble shape, almost like an animal.

"Look!" Becky squeaked. "It's a bird."

"It's a buzzard!" Claire said.

"How is she doing that?" Paisley said.

"It's a raven!" Honey said. The Sleepy Hollow mascot. "It's a raven."

The raven bubble turned its head toward her as though it had heard her. Its eye gleamed wet with bubble soap. With a switch of its tail it began floating closer to her. Honey slowed her swing. What would happen if she hit it? Would it burst like a normal, everyday bubble?

"It's going after Honey," Aiden called. The bird did seem to be floating her direction. It hovered above her swing, its gelatinous body quivered in the breeze. Then like magic, it hardened. Its wings pinned to its side and the raven dived straight down on her. The momentum of Honey's swing carried her up and up towards a collision course with the bird.

"Attack," Clarice called.

Honey threw her hands over her head before impact, sprang from the swing and landed with a thud on the jagged, wood chips.

"Ooo..." Everyone groaned.

"She broke the bird," a girl whined.

Why were they worried about a bird while Honey laid spread out on the ground with wood chips and splinters stuck to her knees and chin? Honey sat up. She felt so many emotions her head spun. She was embarrassed. Angry. Humiliated. Before she was ready, Claire grabbed her by the wrist and hoisted her up.

"No broken bones?" Claire asked. "Then you're ready to fight?"

Becky edged Claire aside. "She isn't going to fight. She skinned her knees."

Her knees didn't hurt nearly as much as her feelings. She saw Clarice strutting across the playground. Honey straightened. She would stand up to Clarice.

142 "What's going on here?" Mrs. Tenure pushed through the kids.

"Honey ruined our bubble game." Clarice pointed at Honey with her bendy wand.

"I was only swinging," Honey said. "You're the one attacking people with bubbles."

Mrs. Tenure looked from Honey to the swing behind her. "Attacking you with bubbles? Honey, bubbles can't hurt anyone."

"It wasn't a normal bubble. It was a killer bubble. It flew over and attacked me." But would

Mrs. Tenure ever believe her? Probably not, because even Honey had trouble believing it.

"It was an amazing bubble," D'Shaunte said. "Clarice worked hard on it, and Honey destroyed it just because it floated near her face."

Clarice let her bottom lip droop like she was the one injured. "All I wanted was to show my friends something cool," she said.

143

Anger burned up Honey's neck. But while she was still framing the best phrases to accurately present her case, Paige threw in her two cents.

"Honey's just jealous. She's mad because we beat her at the jump rope race, and now Clarice is better at bubbles than she is."

Mrs. Tenure put her hand on her hip. "I heard about the jump rope race, Honey. If you don't settle down and stop bullying these girls, I'm going to have a talk with your parents." Honey's mouth dropped open. "But I'm not the bully."

"Make another bubble," Aiden said. "That was really cool."

Clarice adjusted her dark glasses. "I'd love to, but it won't work anymore. Honey broke the magic. She ruined it."

"Way to go, Honey." Aiden rolled his eyes in disgust.

"You should've kept on swinging," Madeline said, "instead of ruining our fun. What a jerk."

144

No matter how much Paisley begged, Madeline wouldn't be joining the Queen Bees now.

"Recess is over," Mrs. Tenure called. "Get back to class."

With ugly looks and rude comments, her classmates filed past on their way back to the building. Becky and Claire stood on either side of Honey, staring down those brave enough to complain to her face.

"How could they blame this on us?" Honey asked as the last kid passed them.

"Clarice is very persuasive," Becky said. "But don't worry. People will see through her fakeness soon. She won't fool them for long."

But how was she fooling people? That's what Honey wanted to know. How was she getting people to do what she wanted? Especially the grown-ups like Miss Fortissimo?

145

146

QUIET PLEASE! PEOPLE ARE READING

LONG OVERDUE

Library day was Honey's favorite day of the week. She usually finished the books she checked out by the weekend, and then began the horrible wait until she could get new ones. If she were lucky her mom would let her make a trip to the city library on Monday to tide her over, but with Mom's work schedule that hadn't happened. Today she could finally get the sequel to the dolphin book Becky had recommended. By tomorrow she and Becky would be discussing Tabby's amazing solution to the latest mystery.

Honey pulled the books from her turtle backpack and got in line with the rest of the class.

"I'm on book twelve," Becky said, "and they keep getting better and better."

"I'm going to get books two, three, four, five and six," Honey said, "since five is the limit."

"You're going to catch me," Becky said. "I'd better read faster if I'm going to stay ahead of you."

The line moved through the hall past the art classroom. From the odor of clay and tempera paints in the hall, Honey would've known where they were with her eyes closed. Then came the smell of new carpet that told her they were in the library. Ever since they'd re-carpeted the library Honey had always thought of books when she smelled new carpet. It had quickly become her favorite smell. Once inside the doors, the kids headed to their favorite section of the library. Claire went to the sports shelf of the non-fiction section. She'd come back to class with another book of workouts and tips for athletes if Mrs. Tenure didn't catch her. According to Mrs. Tenure, she had to read something else for her book reports because Mrs. Tenure was tired of hearing from a ten-year-old how she was abusing her health.

Walker would go check for a new edition of Guinness Book of World Records and Noah reached for the series of books about a boy magician. Honey and Becky walked to the fiction section and each took the copies they were looking for.

"Look who had the nerve to show up." Clarice stood with D'Shaunte and Taylor blocking their way out of the bookcases. "I guess you might as well read since you're no good at races or bubbles."

Honey walked up to Clarice, nose to nose. She opened her mouth like she was going to say something, but instead breathed out a hot, sweaty breath of air right in Clarice's face. Clarice's sunglasses fogged up.

With a scowl, she ripped the shades off. "I've already seen you, Honey Moon. I know what you're capable of. That's why you should join us, or else we'll be your worst nightmare."

"Bring it," Honey said. She stacked her books on top of the bookcase and rolled up her sleeves. "We're the Queen Bees and we aren't afraid of some shady characters."

"You think you can beat us?" Taylor asked. "Let's just see how many friends the Queen Bees have." Taylor turned and walked into the common area of the library. "Excuse me," she called. "Honey Moon has just announced that she's in charge of a club called the Queen Bees. Their claim to fame is cheating at the jump rope race and breaking Clarice's magic bubbles. Does anyone here want to join the Queen Bees?"

"Shhh...." The school librarian had a line of

kids at the circulation desk or she would've physically stopped them. Instead she narrowed her eyes and shushed them.

"That's right," Honey Moon said. "The Queen Bees are looking for more members who are tired of the Royal Shades. Join us and after a brief period of training you will be allowed to be one of us."

"Training?" Aiden called. "What are you training for? How to cheat? How to break toys at recess?"

Claire bounded out of the sports section. "You'd better watch your words, Aiden. The Queen Bees know karate."

"Boys aren't allowed anyway," Honey said, feeling like someone on trial. Eyes were darting between her and the Royal Shades. She had to convince them. "We are so much better than they are. Why would anyone want to be with those losers?"

"That's not very nice," Brianna said.

"But we have a really cute clubhouse," Becky said. "It's all decorated with yellow and black, and as soon as we get more people to sign-up, we'll have more snacks at our meetings."

"Yeah, we have to feed you," Paisley said. "This doesn't sound like a good deal."

"Exactly," Clarice said. "The Queen Bees need some worker bees to keep their hive alive."

152

"Girls!" The librarian was checking out D'Shaunte's stack of books. "Don't make me come over there," she whisper-yelled.

"Can you make magic bubbles?" asked Emily. "Or do you just pop them?"

Finally finished with the line of kids, the librarian stepped between the warring clubs. "I don't know what's gotten into you girls, but you know better than to do this. What gave you the idea it was okay to fight in the library?"

"You have books teaching us how." Claire held up *Learn the Tricks of the Black Belts*.

The librarian shook her head. "Get your books. Mrs. Tenure will be here in five minutes."

"No one wants to be a member of your stinky club," Taylor said as she walked past. "So give it up."

How could everyone think that the Queen Bees were as bad as the Royal Shades? It just didn't make sense. They were the good guys. Couldn't everyone see that?

Honey turned to where she'd left her stack of *Tabby the Dolphin Rescuer* books, but they were gone. Honey walked back to the shelf. She stuck her hand in the gap between books one and seven. They couldn't disappear out of thin air.

Becky followed her to the circulation desk. "I had a stack of books," Honey told the librarian.

"And?" Mrs. Dewey said.

"And they are gone." Ticking off the librarian hadn't been in the plans.

"Are you looking for these?" D'Shaunte produced the stack of books.

Just imagine? A Royal Shade doing something nice for Honey. "Yes, thanks."

"Oh, I'm sorry," D'Shaunte batted her eyelashes. "I just checked these books out."

"What?" Honey flashed a look at Mrs. Dewey. "You knew I was getting those books."

154

"Were you? I found them on the bookshelf while you were talking to Clarice. How was I supposed to know?" D'Shaunte asked.

Mrs. Dewey typed Honey's name into the computer. "I can put you on the waiting list."

Oh, no. It'd be two weeks before D'Shaunte had to turn the books back in. But it could be worse. "OK. Make me the next person on the list."

155

"Well, it's not that simple. These books must be very popular. So far I have Clarice, Paige, and Taylor also on the waiting list. So you should be able to get the books in...two months?"

"Two months? Are you serious?" They'd be on summer break by then. Honey scuffed her tennis shoe against the circulation desk.

These Royal Shades were a royal pain. And Honey's frustration was growing.

Honey tried not to think about the germs that were crawling on every surface. She'd told Mrs. Tenure that she felt sick to her stomach and she wanted to go home. Now she was sitting on the bench like a defendant in the courtroom, waiting for her sentencing. Would Nurse Calamine let her go home, or not?

"You don't have a temperature." Nurse Calamine wrote notes on a piece of paper that would undoubtedly go into Honey's permanent file and keep her from getting a college scholarship. "But we don't want you to vomit in the classroom. Teachers don't appreciate that. I'll call your mom and see if she wants you to come home."

Honey wrapped her arms around her stomach, which had now begun to hurt in earnest. This was the worst day ever. First the playground, then the library—and the library was usually her domain. Defeat on her own turf stung incredibly. She needed to go home. Then she'd feel better.

The curtain next to her bench swayed. The

rings rattled on the track and then it swooshed to the side. Brianna poked her head through the opening. Her blond hair piled on top her head like a messy wedding cake. She had the ruffle from a clown costume around her neck and a red ball stuck on her nose.

"What are you doing here?" Honey asked. "I thought you went to your special class." Lucky Brianna, she got to miss the boring parts of class to study with her tutor. Honey was jealous.

"Today I'm learning about being a nurse," she said. "Sometimes kids are afraid of going to the nurse so I wore my clown outfit to make them feel better."

"That's nice." Honey had to admit seeing Brianna did make her feel better.

"I wanted to tell you that I borrowed Paige's glasses while you were in the library. You aren't so scary anymore. You didn't look any bigger than Jacob or Taylor or any of the other kids."

"Really? I'm not scary anymore?" Honey was disappointed. The paper on the bench crinkled beneath her as she scooted around. "No wonder Clarice isn't afraid of me. But what happened? Why do I look different now?"

Brianna squeezed her nose. It made a honking sound. "Something changed. What were you thinking when you first heard about the Shades?"

158

Forgetting her upset stomach, Honey sat up straight. "I thought that what they were doing wasn't right. They were bullying everyone. They were treating other people like they weren't important. That's what I wanted to stop."

Brianna closed one eye and peered at Honey. "What have you done about it?"

"I made my own club. We're going to fight them. We're going to win, and we'll be a better club because I'll be in charge."

"And everyone will have to obey you? And everyone will do what you order them to do?"

Brianna pulled off her funny nose.

"But I'll tell them to do good stuff," Honey said. "I'll boss them around for their own good."

"That explains it," Brianna said. "You stopped being scary to the Shades when you became like them."

Honey didn't like the sound of that. Brianna wasn't right. Things would be much better at school once the Queen Bees ran the Royal Shades out of business. If Honey had a whole army of fifth-grade girls under her command the world would be a better place.

Brianna shrugged. "I'm just telling you what I saw. Lying to you wouldn't help." Then she popped her clown nose back on and disappeared behind the curtain.

Nurse Calamine hung up the phone. "That was your grandma. She and your brother will be here to get you in a minute."

Honey was feeling better already. She took

her pass from the nurse and walked to the front office. From the window she saw Grandma as soon as she pulled up in her convertible Volkswagen bug.

Harvest waved from his car seat in the back as Honey left the school. Honey opened the door and before she could sit down Grandma handed her a plastic bag.

"Don't puke on my car," she said. Her white hair was held back by a sweatband and she wore a tank top. "Harvest and I were at the park when the nurse called."

Honey tossed her ugly turtle backpack next to Harvest. "It was probably something I ate at lunch. I'm not going to puke."

In no time they were home, and thanks to her visit to the nurse--and Grandma being Grandma--no one said a word about her daily chores. It was about time someone had given her a break. Doing all this work just wasn't fair.

She opened the snack cabinet door. She

stood on her tiptoes and snagged the graham cracker box. And now peanut butter? She searched for her favorite brand, and pulled the new jar off the shelf. Grandma had just buckled Harvest into his highchair when Honey saw a most disturbing sight.

"Crunchy? Who bought crunchy peanut butter?"

Grandma tousled Harvest's hair. "My guess is your mom. Pass those graham crackers."

161

Honey slid the jar across the table top and flopped into a chair. "She knows I don't like crunchy. And this brand? It's the cheap stuff. I work hard around here. Don't I deserve the best? I'm the president of the Queen Bees. Crunchy peanut butter is not fit for a Queen."

Her grandmother raised an eyebrow. "Someone's getting a little big for her britches." If Grandma only knew what Honey was up against at school, she might take her more seriously. Instead she continued with her lecture.

162

"What makes you think you deserve your favorite peanut butter, Honey Moon? Did you pay for it? Did you take your time going to the store and buying the groceries? Geez, Louise. What are they teaching kids nowadays. When I was a kid—"

"I don't need the snack," Honey said. "Becky is bringing something."

"Suit yourself," Grandma said.

Grown-ups just didn't understand the pressures that fifth-grade girls lived with. Grown-ups just went to work, did their chores, worked in the yard on Saturday, and went to church on Sunday. They didn't even know the meaning of the word stress. How could they when they lived such a tame, protected life?

Honey opened up the shed and took her throne. At least here was one place she could get away from all the bossy people who treated her like a child, but expected her to work like an adult. She reached over to flip the switch on what was left of the yellow and black flower pot lights. The shed mellowed with the golden spotlights coming down. No one would take her library books here. No one would attack her with killer bubbles while she was in her own clubhouse.

And she wouldn't have to eat crunchy peanut butter because Becky was her best friend and she knew what kind of snacks Honey liked.

Speaking of Becky, she popped her head around the corner. "There you are," she said.

163

Then hollered to Claire, "She's in the clubhouse. No use ringing the doorbell."

Honey looked at Becky's empty hands. "Where are the cookies?"

Becky twisted a curl around her finger. "You said I had to bring snacks while I was in training. Now I'm a full member."

"Yeah, me too," Claire said.

164

"Then who is going to bring the snacks?" Honey asked. "And where's Paisley?"

"She dropped out. Too much pressure at school."

"We have to recruit new members," Becky answered. "That's all."

"Yeah and they have to get serious about cleaning up around the place." Claire dropped into her lawn chair. "Becky and I don't have to clean anymore."

Honey looked around. Some leaves had blown in under the door. There was a new spider web in the corner and they'd left some candy wrappers on the floor. Not only that, but Claire had forgotten to take her leftover cookies home last time. Honey licked her lips. Seven chocolate chip cookies were stacked on a plate that'd been pushed in the corner. Two for each of them and a spare. Exactly what they were looking for.

"Claire," she said. "Hand me that plate. We have a snack after all."

"I'm not sure..." Becky said.

Claire picked up the plate. Holding it level to her eyes she squinted. "Who left a half-eaten cookie? You don't eat half a cookie—" She screamed and launched the plate over her head scattering the cookies all over.

"What are you doing?" Honey yelled as cookies rained down on them. But then she saw a blur in the corner. A furry blur that skimmed along the edge of the clubhouse.

"Mice!" Claire screamed. "I moved the plate and there were mice. I hate mice." She shivered.

Becky followed them calmly. "They are just mice."

"I almost shared a cookie with a rat," Honey said. "Who forgot to clean the shed?"

"We don't have to clean the shed," Claire shot back. "We're Queen Bees. We're important. Let someone else clean it up."

"But if no one cleans it, then we won't have anything nice," Honey said. "Someone has to do the work." But even as she said it, she got the sinking feeling that she'd had the conversation once before. Except she'd been on the other side of the argument.

CHAOS IN CHOIR

They didn't have a clubhouse anymore. Not one they could go into. Ever since they'd all graduated to full members, and the mice had taken over. Honey couldn't live with mice.

But she didn't like loud noise either, so she should've found a way to avoid music class, too.

The next day, music class had gotten out of hand before it had even started. Today they'd entered the music room to find percussion instruments lining the back wall. If the smartest thing to do was to dash to the instruments and try to make as much noise as possible before Miss Fortissimo stopped you, then Honey's class was filled with geniuses.

Cymbals smashed, drums thudded, bells rung and triangles did what triangles do. Honey covered her ears. Of all the instruments, the marimba looked the most interesting to Honey. She found a small, hard mallet, and ran it up and down the tone bars making a rainbow of music.

The classroom door slammed shut. Miss Fortissimo's hair fuzzed out in every direction. But instead of immediately taking control, she slunk to the piano bench. Honey shot a look at Becky, but Becky was too busy making tinkling music with chimes to notice.

Miss Fortissimo had warned Honey about messing with the Royal Shades, but she needed help. Maybe this was Honey's chance to bring Miss Fortissimo around to their side.

Honey approached. "Miss Fortissimo, er..." She didn't want to point out that no teacher in their right mind would leave percussion instruments out. How to say it gently? "Thank you for letting us play with the drums. Everyone is having lots of fun."

Miss Fortissimo trailed her long necklace through her fingers. "I'm going to lose my job, so it doesn't matter now."

Honey frowned. She sat next to her on the bench. "What's wrong?"

"When Clarice's class was here, she insisted that I let them get the drums out. I didn't want to, but I gave in. Next thing I knew they were marching around the room. I couldn't believe she'd even ask to do that, but every class she's been bossier and bossier. When I said 'no' she flew into a rage." Miss Fortissimo's face looked pale. "She's trying to ruin me."

"I don't understand," Honey said. "Why are you afraid of her? She's just a kid."

"She's the mayor's daughter, and she's not just a kid. She's dark and scary. Those glasses..." Miss Fortissimo shuddered.

Honey nearly jumped off the bench when the cymbals crashed. Cheering kids laughed and a chair overturned, but Miss Fortissimo didn't notice any of it. Honey moved closer. "What do you know about the glasses?"

Miss Fortissimo looked hard at Honey. "You're going to think I'm crazy. One day I was in here alone and Clarice came in. She told me that I wouldn't believe how good I'd look in these glasses. Well, I'd just got my hair colored so I was anxious to see what she was talking about. I put them on and stood in front of the mirror." Miss Fortissimo shuddered. "I wish I'd never seen my reflection. I looked small and puny. My skin looked fake, my mouth grotesque. I looked like a weak, diseased version of myself. I'd be so ashamed if anyone saw me looking like that."

Honey's mind whirled. She had looked scary, until she'd gone and started acting like a jerk. Maybe the message Clarice saw in her glasses this time was that Miss Fortissimo could be easily bullied.

"What you saw isn't the truth," Honey said. "I've talked to someone who wore the glasses and people can change. You can change. You don't have to be weak."

"But she said if I stand up against her she'll tell Mr. Chancellor and her dad what I'm really like. That's probably where she was headed when she left last period."

171

Honey looked at the clock. Last period had ended five minutes ago. Five minutes of complete chaos for her fifth-grade class to bang away at will. Did they have time to pull it together before they got caught?

Honey jumped up. "Hey," she yelled. No one stopped. She stood on the piano bench.

"Hey!!" No one could hear her over the ruckus

of the drums. She was desperate. She took one more step up, right on the piano keyboard.

Brunk! Crunk! Kerplunk! Honey stomped all the way from middle C to the bass clef.

"Be quiet!"

The class stopped. Even Miss Fortissimo sat with her mouth opened as she looked at Honey's dirty sneakers on her ivories.

"Look," Honey said. "I know I'm bossy, but if you could do this, it would help Miss Fortissimo, not me. We need to get all the drums back in the closet and then line up on the risers before Mr. Chancellor catches us."

The room was silent. Becky and Brianna looked at each other. They took opposite sides of the marimba and rolled it to the supply closet. That snapped the rest of the class into action.

"Hey, Aiden," Claire called. "Hold that bucket up."

Aiden lifted the container than held the mallets and drumsticks and Claire began tossing them into it from across the room. Honey ran to the door and peered out the narrow window. Just as promised, here came Clarice with Mr. Chancellor. Honey spun to Miss Fortissimo.

"Don't be little," she said. "Be brave. You have kindness and goodness in you. Show it." Honey handed Miss Fortissimo some music. "Play something."

The kids scrambled to the risers when the

music started. By the time the door opened they were belting out,

"We wish you a spooky Christmas. We wish you a spooky Christmas. We wish you a spooky Christmas, and a terrifying New Year."

"Why did you pick that song?" Becky asked. "It's May."

"I just grabbed some music," Honey said. "I didn't read it."

Miss Fortissimo finished the chorus with a flourish on the piano. "Mr. Chancellor, how nice of you to visit us."

"Clarice was concerned that your class was in disarray." Mr. Chancellor rubbed his saggy belly. "It seems that everything is satisfactory, now."

Unless you believed that Christmas carols should only be sung in December. Besides that—

"It is," Miss Fortissimo said.

"Instead of recess," Mr. Chancellor said, "I think Clarice and her class would benefit from study hall for their behavior. I'll make sure their teacher is advised."

Clarice's chin got all hard and pointy. She showed her teeth, which made her look a lot like her thug of a big brother, Titus. "You think I don't know what you did?" she told Honey. "You just wait. You're going to be the most hated person in the fifth grade."

Maybe, but Honey had learned one thing. Sometimes, popular people weren't nice and sometimes nice people weren't popular. It was up to Honey to do what was right and face the consequences.

"Mom, I'm home." Honey tossed her backpack on the table and headed to the fridge. She felt good about helping Miss Fortissimo, but what would it cost her? Would Clarice make good on her threats? Would her own Queen Bees turn against her and leave her to sit by herself at lunch?

She reached for the fridge handle and stopped. Something had changed. There was a different letter from Anisha stuck to the fridge door.

Anisha's letter had the same picture attached to the top of it. Her bright green dress looked like a long scarf wrapped around her waist and thrown over one shoulder.

176

Dear Moon family,

I'm sorry to tell you that my school is closed. There is a sickness. So far I am not sick. Pray that I can stay healthy. School will reopen when officials allow it. Until then I help my family and make extra money. I will grind spices in the village if I am lucky.

Love,
Anisha

Grinding spices? According to Honey's parents, kids like Anisha had to work hard to have rice to eat. Her stomach wobbled as she grabbed a yogurt. Honey's eyes drifted to her chore chart. Today she had to fold two loads of laundry and put the clothes up. It would take her less than half an hour. Folding a stack of laundry? So much better than sitting on the ground grinding spices all day, every day, with no TV, no air conditioning. Anisha would probably eat crunchy peanut butter, too, without crying that she deserved better.

Honey skipped to the laundry room and unloaded the warm pile of clothes into the hamper. She buried her nose into the towels and breathed in the flowery scent. After switching the wet clothes to the dryer, she carried the hamper into the living room and dumped it on the couch.

She'd barely got the first towel folded when her doorbell rang. It was Claire and Becky.

"More stinky chores?" Claire dropped into the recliner and kicked her feet over the edge of the chair.

"Actually this chore smells good," Honey said.

Becky slid a tin of cookies on the ottoman. "I'll help you. Then we can clean out the club house. I brought some little traps that catch the mice without hurting them, so we can release them somewhere else."

"Great idea," Honey said. "But this is my

work. It doesn't hurt me to do it."

Becky smiled. "Then maybe you won't mind what I'm getting ready to say. Since we've stood strong and have stopped the Royal Shades from bossing everyone around, I thought the Queen Bees could tackle another project. What if we looked for people to help? What if instead of signing up members so they can do what we tell them, what if we help people, even if they aren't our members?"

"I bet I'm a better helper than either one of you." Claire stood up and put both fists into the air. "I'm the best helper, ever."

179

Honey pounded her fist on a stack of towels. "That's exactly what I was thinking," she said. "We could use our club house to talk about the things we want to do. And we can invite people that need a friend. You never know who else Clarice Kligore has been bullying."

It was a plan. From then on the Queen Bees would be more about their work and less about their sting.

180

WEEDING OUT
THE COMPETITION

After the school bell rang the next day, Honey headed straight for the back entrance of the school where the cars lined up for the kids who were lucky enough to get a ride home. Today Honey was lucky. Grandma was watching Harvest again and had told Honey to plan for a trip to the park.

"I'm glad your mom has you. Don't know how your mother gets it all done," Grandma said as Honey climbed in. "Harvest keeps me running all day, every day. Your mom works all day and then comes home to a house messed up by Hurricane Harvest. How does she keep up?"

Honey looked out the window. Sometimes she thought it was because she did all the work. But that wasn't true. Her short list of chores didn't even take care of all the trouble she caused. If no laundry was washed, no trash taken out, how long would it be before clothes were piled in the corner? How long before rats darted through the garbage? Someone had to do it.

"It's a gorgeous day," Grandma said, "and I can't wait to get some sun on my shoulders, but that will mean that I'll need your help with Harvest when we get back to the house. I want to put dinner on before your parents get home."

"I'll help you," Honey said. "After all, I'm going to be eating the food too."

"Park!" Harvest cheered and kicked the back of Honey's seat. Grandma turned a sharp right and headed down Claire's street to where the park was. Honey watched the houses go by. She knew this street well because she and Becky had ridden their bikes up and down it a million times. They approached a neat, blue house with white trim and messy flower beds, but freshly mown grass.

"Stop!" Honey said. "Stop the car!"

Grandma hit her brakes. They skidded to a stop.

"That's Mrs. Wilcox's mother's house." Honey looked at the weeds among the flowers. "I know you want to go to the park," she said, "but do you think we could clean out her flower beds first? You'll still get sun on your shoulders."

Harvest didn't look happy. "What do you think, Harvest?" Grandma asked. "Let's help and then we'll get ice cream."

183

At the words ice cream, Harvest clapped. If only everyone was as easy to please. Honey unfastened her seatbelt and soon she, Grandma, and Harvest were getting their hands dirty.

Honey's knees pressed into the cool, green grass. She tugged up a thick, rough weed with a dagger-shaped root. "Look at that," she said.

Grandma nodded. "I'm impressed. You are sure we're at the right house, aren't you? I'd hate for a stranger to come out and catch us tearing their dirt apart."

"I don't think they'll mind," Honey said. The door creaked open.

"Honey? Harvest? Mrs. Moon? What are you doing?" Mrs. Wilcox called.

"We're fixing your flower beds," Honey said. "We don't want you or your mom to worry about it."

"Well, Honey, I've never heard of anything so kind." She bent to pick up Harvest who was begging for her attention. "Every little bit you can do will help. I know Mom hates thinking about how overgrown it's gotten."

"About those roses," Grandma said. "If you have some clippers I'd be happy to prune them."

Just as Grandma and Mrs. Wilcox left to get some tools, Honey saw Becky and Claire walking down the street.

"I thought you were going to the park," Claire said.

"We were, but then I remembered Mrs. Wilcox's mother and her yard and the flowers."

"Can we help?" Becky asked.

Honey grabbed another weed by the stem. "There's plenty to do."

"I'll drop my stuff off at home," Becky said. "And I'll be right back."

Claire tossed her book bag to the ground and squatted right in the middle of the flower bed. "I bet I can pull weeds fast. I have great eye/hand dexterity."

Claire was always trying to win a contest and at times that helped a lot. But she jerked the weed so hard that it flew out of the ground and threw dirt all over Honey's face.

Honey kept her eyes closed while she wiped the dirt away.

"Sorry," Claire said. "I didn't mean to do that."

"It's okay." By the time Honey brushed away enough that she could open her eyes she saw Paisley and Madeline standing there.

"The lady who lives here is really nice," Paisley said. "She gives whole candy bars on Halloween."

"She's been sick," Honey explained. "That's why we're fixing her yard."

"Can we help?" Madeline asked.

"You aren't Queen Bees," Claire said. "First you have to submit your application. After that you'll go through the selection process—"

"Yes, you can help," interrupted Honey.

"But they aren't part of the club," Claire said as she tossed a weed over her shoulder.

"Do you think someone has to be a part of our club before they can do good?"

187

Kids continued to walk by making their way home from school. Most passed on without saying anything, but a few stopped to help Mrs. Wilcox's mom.

And then there were those who came for other reasons.

"Hey, come back here!" Clarice yelled.

Honey turned to see Brianna running full speed down the sidewalk. Her clown ruffle bounced with every step. Behind her was Clarice Kligore, chasing her for all she was worth.

"Give those back," Clarice said. "They don't belong to you."

Brianna skidded to a stop directly in front of the yard. Quick as lightning she slid on the pair of black glasses and looked directly at Honey. Then with a big smile she gave her a thumbs up.

"You're big again." She cheered. "As big and scary as ever!"

Clarice caught up with her and ripped the glasses off. "Mind your own business," she said. Then spun around and stomped away.

Honey's heart filled with joy. Doing something for someone else already made her feel better, but now she knew the secret to keeping the royal shades in the dark. It wasn't by being as mean and bossy as they were. It was by serving. As long as they were helping other people, the Queen Bees couldn't lose.

190

SHOWDOWN

Before the bell rang at school the next day, Clarice and the Royal Shades had met under the shady oak in front of the school. Honey wasn't close enough to hear what she said, but she wasn't happy. Paige had her head bowed as Clarice yelled. D'Shaunte stood with her arms crossed, and even Taylor acted like she wanted to be anywhere else but there. The sisterhood of the Royal Shades had begun to crack, just like all friendships built on jealousy and pride.

But it wasn't until lunch that the cracks turned into breaks. The line was moving slow because Miss Fortissimo was setting up the sound equipment for an assembly later that afternoon. Brianna made it past the stage and through the line first. Her long hair was braided and pinned up like a blond Princess Leia. She sat at an empty table. It happened to be the table Clarice and her gang always sat at.

The Shades got their food and followed Clarice to the table. Clarice stopped. Paige walked around her and sat. D'Shaunte went to her seat. Taylor set her tray down, but Clarice didn't move.

"What are you doing at our table?" Clarice's lip turned down in a sneer.

Brianna smiled. "Eating."

Honey had her tray now. So did Claire. Everyone who was still in line was watching.

"Leave," Clarice said. "This is our table."

Brianna rubbed the table with her thumb. "It doesn't have your name on it," she said. "I looked."

"If you look through my glasses, you'll see things differently," Clarice said.

"I've looked through your glasses," Brianna said. "And I saw you. If I was you, I'd get rid of those as fast as you can."

Clarice's face turned red. The silverware on her tray rattled. "Leave!" Clarice said.

Paige stood. "I like Brianna. Why can't she sit with us?"

"She can if she'll join us." Clarice set her tray down.

"And obey you? You know what? I'm done with this." Paige took her glasses off. She blinked like the light hurt her eyes. Then she turned the glasses over in her hand and looked at them. "I don't ever want to wear these again." She dropped them on the floor, then with a crunch, smashed them to bits.

Honey's jaw dropped open. Never in a hundred years did she think that one of the Shades would do something nice. But now she knew what she had to do. She knew she was right where she needed to be.

Paige left the shady table, while Clarice seethed. "You can sit with us," Honey said.

"Do I have to join another club?" Paige asked.

"No," Honey said. "We're just some girls hanging out. Anyone can sit with us."

Paige scooted in next to Becky, who was beaming. Honey looked to D'Shaunte. "You can sit here too."

D'Shaunte looked around the cafeteria. "I want to sit with Emily. I haven't talked to her since I joined this stupid club." She tossed her glasses in the can full of nasty lunchroom trash.

"That'll go to the trash compactor," Honey said. "Two down, two to go."

"You aren't getting our glasses," Clarice said. "Taylor and I are partners to the end."

"Well," said Taylor. "I am getting tired of pretending like everyone else is our enemies. So if you don't mind..."

She took off her glasses, but before she could crunch them, Clarice grabbed them out of her hand. "I'll start a new club. There'll only be two of us, but we'll rule the school. I'll find the perfect person to join me...there!" Clarice ran to the stage where Miss Fortissimo was working and stuck the glasses on her. Miss Fortissimo froze. She started chewing her lip, but she didn't take the glasses off. "I don't need kids," Clarice said, "when I can have a teacher do my dirty work."

Miss Fortissimo looked as frightened as a kindergartner standing in front of the Headless Horseman. But if it wasn't Miss Fortissimo, it'd be someone else. Sooner or later Clarice would

195

find someone who could be frightened into doing her bidding. And with her magic glasses she'd know exactly who lacked the backbone to stand up to her.

Be brave, Honey Moon. Be brave.

Honey raced down the aisle between the long rows of chairs. Passing the sound board she threw a switch, then jumped on the stage. With a yank she got the microphone out of the stand and found the on button.

"If you are wearing any kind of glasses, take them off." Honey's voice echoed through the now silent cafeteria. "Hold your hands over the lenses." She didn't know where she got this idea, but she hoped it worked.

"These glasses are more powerful than you," Clarice shrieked. "I'm not taking them off."

Miss Fortissimo was helpless.

Honey looked around the room. Everyone was in the clear. "Here it goes," she said. Then she moved toward the speaker with the microphone held out in front of her.

"WWWHHHEEEEE...." The speaker screeched. The kids all groaned and covered their ears. Some of them put their head under the table. The noise was deafening, but Honey couldn't cover her ears and hold the microphone at the same time. She walked closer. The pitch went higher and higher, until she thought her eardrums would burst. She could only get a little closer. Squinting in pain, Honey pushed the microphone right up against the speaker box. She was doing this for Miss Fortissimo, for Paige, for Brianna, for all the people that Clarice would bully.

197

Miss Fortissimo gave a sharp laugh as the lenses on the glasses cracked, and then fell apart. Something in the trashcan exploded, sending a tiny puff of French fries up in the air. Only Clarice's glasses were left.

Ping! Ping! The glasses blew out. Her eyes were framed by the empty rims. They flashed with anger, but there were no more glasses to worry about. Honey had saved the day.

The screeching suddenly stopped. Miss Fortissimo waved at Honey from behind the sound board. She'd turned off the microphone, but Honey still couldn't hear anything she said. The only noise Honey noticed was the ringing in her ears.

From the pats on her back, Honey could tell that she'd accomplished something grand. Even Taylor mouthed something about being sorry before she ran to the playground. But Clarice was nowhere to be found. Claire claimed that she saw her father's long black car, the one they called the Phantom Lustro, picking her up before recess was even over. She didn't come back that day.

Honey skipped all the way home after school. Mom had worked an early shift, so she was in the kitchen working on her laptop when Honey walked through the door.

Mom stuck her finger on a line of the bank statement before she looked up. "You seem like you're in a good mood. How was school?"

"The best." Honey said.

Mom smiled. "You don't have to shout."

"I'm shouting?" Yeah, probably. That ringing in her ears hadn't gone away yet. "We beat the Royal Shades. They aren't going to be bugging people, anymore."

"So the Queen Bees rule the hive?"

"The Queen Bees are retiring. Our mission has been accomplished." Honey took the jug of orange juice out of the refrigerator. This time she'd use a cup.

199

"I thought that being a part of a club made you feel important," Mom said. "You could have a special group of friends."

Honey looked at Anisha's picture. "I guess I figured out that everyone is important. God didn't make people that don't matter to Him. And if you want to be special, well, there are different kinds of special. But the best kind of special is the kind that stands up for what is right. Those are the kind of friends I want."

Mom completely lost her place on her

bank statement. "You are special to us, more than any other little girl in the world." She pulled Honey to her with a side hug.

Honey wrapped her arm around her mother's shoulder. "You can have the garden shed back, too. We won't be meeting in it anymore. I'll get our stuff cleaned out in a minute. First, I have to do my chores."

"Another special thing you can do."

"Nope." Honey set her glass in the sink. "Cleaning up and helping out isn't special. It's just part of life. Not a part of life that I'm really excited about..."

"Honey Moon, you'd better watch it." But Mom was smiling.

Honey ran her fingers over the gold stars on her paper, said a prayer for Anisha, then ran off to finish her chores. Then it would be on to her next quest. To go wherever she was needed.

201

CREATOR'S NOTES

I am enchanted with the world of Honey Moon, the younger sister of Harry Moon. She is smart and courageous and willing to do anything to help right win out. What a powerhouse.

I wish I had a friend like Honey when I was in school. There is something cool about the way Honey and her friends connect with each other that's very special. When I was Honey's age, I spent most of my time in our family barn taking care of rabbits and didn't hang out with other kids a lot. I think I was always a little bit on the outside.

Maybe that's why I like Honey so much. She lives life with wonderful energy and enthusiasm. She doesn't hesitate to speak her mind. And she demands that adults pay attention to her because more often than not, the girl knows what she is talking about. And she often finds herself getting into all kinds of crazy adventures.

We all need real friends like Honey. Growing up is quite an adventure and living it with girlfriends that you love builds friendships that can last a lifetime. That's the point, I think, of Honey's enchanted world — life is just better when you work it out with friends.

I am happy that you have decided to join me, along with author Regina Jennings, in the enchanted world of Honey Moon. I would love for you to let us know about any fun ideas you have for Honey in her future stories. Visit harrymoon.com and let us know.

See you again in our next visit to the enchanted world of Honey Moon!

MARK ANTHONY POE

203

The Enchanted World of Honey Moon creator Mark Andrew Poe never thought about creating a town where kids battled right and wrong. His dream was to love and care for animals, specifically his friends in the rabbit community.

Along the way, Mark became successful in all sorts of interesting careers. He entered the print and publishing world as a young man and his company did really, really well. Mark also became a popular and nationally sought-after health care advocate for the care and well-being of rabbits.

Years ago, Mark came up with the idea of a story about a young boy with a special connection to a world of magic, all revealed through a remarkable rabbit friend. Mark worked on his idea for several years before building a collaborative creative team to help him bring his idea to life.

Harry Moon was born. The team was thrilled when Mark introduced Harry's enchanting sister, Honey Moon. Boy, did she pack an unexpected punch!

In 2014, Mark began a multi-book project to launch *The Amazing Adventures of Harry Moon* and *The Enchanted World of Honey Moon* into the youth marketplace. Harry and Honey are kids who understand the difference between right and wrong. Kids who tangle with magic and forces unseen in a town where "every day is Halloween night." Today, Mark and the creative team continue to work on the many stories of Harry and Honey and the characters of Sleepy Hollow. He lives in suburban Chicago with his wife and his 25 rabbits.

SUZANNE BROOKS KUHN

Suzanne Brooks Kuhn is a mom and author with a passion for children's stories. Suzanne brings her precocious childhood experiences and sassy storytelling ability to her creative team in weaving the magical stories found in *The Enchanted World of Honey Moon*. Suzanne lives with her husband in an 1800's farmhouse nestled in the countryside of central Virginia.

205

BE SURE TO READ THE
CONTINUING AND ENCHANTED
ADVENTURES OF HONEY MOON.

HONEY MOON 🌑 BOOK CLUB

Become a member of the
Honey Moon Book Club and receive another
of Honey's adventures every other month
along with a bag full of goodies!

Skip over to www.harrymoon.com
and sign up today.

ALSO IN THE HONEY MOON LIBRARY:

THE ENCHANTED WORLD OF HONEY MOON

A SCARY LITTLE CHRISTMAS

Suzanne Brooks Kuhn   Created by Mark Andrew Poe

THE ENCHANTED WORLD OF HONEY MOON

NOT YOUR VALENTINE

Suzanne Brooks Kuhn   Created by Mark Andrew Poe

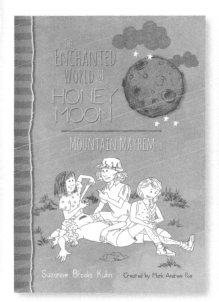

THE ENCHANTED WORLD OF HONEY MOON

MOUNTAIN MAYHEM

Suzanne Brooks Kuhn   Created by Mark Andrew Poe

THE ENCHANTED WORLD OF HONEY MOON

SCARY SMART HOUSE

Suzanne Brooks Kuhn   Created by Mark Andrew Poe

Dear Diary: _____

Dear Diary: _____

_____

_____

_____

_____

_____

_____

_____

209

_____

_____

_____

_____

_____

_____

_____

_____

_____

_____

_____

Dear Diary: _____

Dear Diary: _____

211

Dear Diary: _____